Critical Guides to Spanish Texts

47 Galdós: Marianela

Critical Guides to Spanish Texts

EDITED BY J.E. VAREY AND A.D. DEYERMOND

PÉRÉZ GALDÓS

Marianela

Geraldine M. Scanlon

Lecturer in Spanish
King's College, London

Grant & Cutler Ltd *in association with*
Tamesis Books Ltd 1988

© Grant & Cutler Ltd
1988
ISBN 0 7293 0282 2

4

333478

I.S.B.N. 84-599-2543-9

DEPÓSITO LEGAL: V. 2.672 - 1988

Printed in Spain by
Artes Gráficas Soler, S.A., Valencia
for
GRANT AND CUTLER LTD
55-57 GREAT MARLBOROUGH STREET, LONDON W1V 2AY

Contents

To the memory of my mother and father

Preface

There are many editions of the novel but none is wholly reliable, and there is no critical edition which takes into account the differences between the manuscript and the various editions. Only editions with a critical analysis and notes are listed in the Bibliographical Note (Section F). The edition I have used, and to which page-references are given, is Benito Pérez Galdós, *Obras completas*, edited by Federico Sainz de Robles, 7th ed., IV (Madrid: Aguilar, 1969), 702-75. Chapter numbers in roman numerals are followed by page numbers in arabic numerals, thus: I, 703. References to non-fictional writings by Galdós, unless otherwise stated, are from volume VI, 5th ed. (1968). Figures in parentheses in italic type refer to the Bibliographical Note; where necessary they are followed by page numbers, thus: *18*, p. 135. Without attempting a detailed comparison I have on occasion drawn on the manuscript version of *Marianela* in this study. A version of Chapter 3 was given as a paper at the III Congreso Internacional Galdosiano held in Las Palmas in August 1985.

I should like to express my gratitude to the staff of the Casa-Museo Galdós for their assistance and to Professor Hensley C. Woodbridge for providing bibliographical material.

Abbreviations

AG   *Anales Galdosianos*

CHA   *Cuadernos Hispanoamericanos*

PMLA   *Publications of the Modern Language Association of America*

RC   *Revista Contemporánea*

1 Introduction

Marianela has always been one of Galdós's most popular novels: first published in 1878, it was reprinted in the same year and then serialized in 43 instalments throughout 1880 and 1881 in the magazine *La Guirnalda*. The numerous subsequent editions, translations, and adaptations for the theatre, opera, cinema and television all testify to the breadth and continuity of its appeal.[1] This success undoubtedly owes much to the tenderness and delicacy of feeling with which Galdós tells the story of Marianela. Yet it is these very qualities which, as Galdós's contemporaries were quick to point out, make *Marianela* something of an exception in his work. Emilia Pardo Bazán remarked that it was 'un género aparte, puesto que ni de política, ni de historia trata; es un drama psicológico, una narración de sentimiento' (*32*, p. 412); Manuel de la Revilla commented 'si en otras novelas sabe hacer pensar, en ésta ha conseguido hacer sentir, por tan delicado modo que pocos poetas pueden envidiarle' (*33*, p. 509). Other contemporaries welcomed this apparent departure from weighty historical, political and religious themes: José María Pereda enthusiastically wrote to Galdós 'a la legua se conoce que no ha querido V. hacer una obra de empeño, sino un entreplato sabroso, delicado' and Ramón Mesonero Romanos praised the novel as 'un idilio de amor de sencillez de ternura'.[2] So unusual is the intensity of the emotion that it has even been suggested that the novel was an attempt by Galdós to exorcise the painful memories of his frustrated youthful passion for his cousin Sisita (*20*, p. 73; *11*, II, p. 287). Be that as it may, it is certainly true that despite the fact that Galdós

[1] See Jean-François Botrel, 'Le Succès d'édition des oeuvres de Benito Pérez Galdós: essai de bibliométrie', *Anales de Literatura Española*, 3 (1984), 119-57, & 4 (1985), 29-66. For editions and translations see Miguel Hernández Suárez, pp. 65-76 (Bibliographical Note, A). The novel has been translated into German, Czechoslovak, English, Finnish, French, Italian and Rumanian. In 1916 it was adapted for the theatre by Serafín and Joaquín Alvarez Quintero, whose version provided the basis for an opera (1923) by Jaime Pahissa; there was a Catalan adaptation and Cuban film and television versions as early as 1931 and 1953 respectively (*26*, II, p. 86). For the more recent operatic version by Benjamín Gutiérrez Sáenz, see Vernon A. Chamberlin, '*Marianela*: The First Costa Rican Opera (1957)', *AG*, 19 (1984), 147-50.

[2] *Cartas a Galdós*, ed. Soledad Ortega (Madrid: Revista de Occidente, 1964), pp. 68 and 30.

with his accustomed modesty dismissed the novel as 'un verdadero adefesio',[3] it had a special significance for him, as is demonstrated by the well-known anecdote of how he broke down and wept during a performance of the dramatized version (*7*, 440-42).

It was, however, evident to the most perspicacious of Galdós's contemporaries that *Marianela* was not simply a love story but an invitation to meditate on serious moral, social and philosophical problems of the day (*31*, *33*). Most modern critics too have argued convincingly that notwithstanding its atypical sentimental tone, *Marianela*, far from being merely a lyrical interlude, is permeated by preoccupations common to Galdós's other novels of the period and also provides a foretaste of the concerns of his later work.

Galdós began writing *Marianela* on 6 December 1877 and sent the manuscript to the printer on 21 January 1878. It belongs to a group of four novels about contemporary life published in the late 1870s –*Doña Perfecta* (1876), *Gloria* (1876-77) and *La familia de León Roch* (1878)– which Galdós subsequently classified as 'Novelas de la primera época'. Until 1876, apart from the short fantasy novel, *La sombra* (1871), Galdós had devoted himself to historical themes: in his first two full-length novels, *La Fontana de Oro* (1870) and *El Audaz* (1871), he had dealt with the years 1820-23 and 1804 respectively; in 1873 with *Trafalgar* he embarked on a more systematic fictional account of the history of Spain from the War of Independence to the triumph of political liberalism in 1834. By 1879 he had published twenty novels, or 'Episodios nacionales', in two series of ten.

It had been the turbulent events of the years following the Revolution of 1868 which had prompted Galdós to turn to the past in an attempt to understand the historical origins of the problems of the present. Initially he had welcomed the Revolution with enthusiasm and supported its programme of political and economic liberalism, faith in education and material progress, anti-militarism and anti-clericalism. The ideological content of the Revolution was to a large extent provided by an intellectual élite which had been formed between 1854 and 1868 under the guidance of Julián Sanz del Río,

[3]Carmen Bravo Villasante, 'Veintiocho cartas de Galdós a Pereda', *CHA*, 250-52 (1970-71), 9-51 (p. 28).

a philosophy professor at the University of Madrid, who had introduced into Spain the ideas of Karl Friedrich Krause, a minor post-Kantian idealist. Krausism effected a complete renovation of ideas in the intellectually stagnant atmosphere of the 1850s and 1860s but the actual details of the philosophy — 'el racionalismo armónico' — were less important than the general values and attitudes which it promoted, in particular a respect for science and reason and an emphasis on ethics (*2*, pp. 48-53). Galdós himself was never a Krausist but he was personally acquainted with, and admired, many of the leading Krausist intellectuals, some of whom had taught him at the university. He was sympathetic to the Krausists' aspirations to intellectual and ethical renewal and shared many of their attitudes: a belief in gradual progess and in the reform of the individual as a prerequisite for the reform of society, the view that the individual conscience should serve as a guide to conduct, a respect and tolerance for the ideas of others, and the conviction that literature should make a serious contribution to the cause of progress. Like the Krausists, Galdós was particularly concerned with religion, the family, the role of women, education and the social problem.

The hopes entertained by Galdós and other liberal intellectuals that the 1868 Revolution would fundamentally regenerate the life of the nation gradually turned sour as the widely disparate aspirations of the different political groups who had made the Revolution led to extreme political instability and frequent changes of government. Galdós's articles on domestic politics written for the *Revista de España* in 1871-72 betray his disillusionment as he saw opportunites for political and social development being squandered because of self-interest and political extremism.[4] The difficulties of reconciling progress and order were exacerbated in the months following the establishment of the First Republic in February 1873 when the régime came under threat from both the reactionary traditionalists who had initiated the second Carlist War in the North, and the federal republican extremists on the left who had provoked cantonalist uprisings in the Levant and the South. The revolutionary *sexenio* —

---

[4]See Benito Pérez Galdós, *Los artículos políticos en la 'Revista de España'*, *1871-1872*, ed. Brian J. Dendle and Joseph Schraibman (Lexington: Dendle & Schraibman, 1982) and Peter B. Goldman, 'Galdós and the Politics of Conciliation', *AG*, 4 (1969), 73-87.

the six years of radical political experiment inaugurated by the Revolution of 1868 — were finally brought to an end on 29 December 1874 by a coup by General Martínez Campos which restored the Bourbon monarchy in the person of Alfonso XII.

In the early years of the Restoration a series of repressive measures — restrictions on freedom of expression, limitation of academic freedom, the suspension of left-wing papers — and the elaboration of the conservative constitution of 1876 made many liberals fear a return to the arbitrary and reactionary régime which had preceded the Revolution of 1868. Such fears and a disillusionment with the results of the revolutionary *sexenio* clearly inform *Doña Perfecta*, *Gloria* and *La familia de León Roch*, all of which are concerned with the problem which lay at the root of the failure of the 1868 Revolution: the difficulties of introducing progressive ideas into a backward society. The novels are structured around a polarization between the protagonists who represent reason, progress, science, moral probity, that is, the reforming idealism of the 1868 Revolution, and society which is superstitious, backward, fanatical and hypocritical. Galdós focuses his attack on the forces of reaction which defeat the hero, but he is not an uncritical spokesman for progressive liberalism: he also explores how the weaknesses of his heroes — presumption, underestimation of the opposition, lack of realism — contribute to their own downfall. This critical perspective reflects in part the increasingly widespread distrust of the abstract idealism which had inspired the attempts at reform during the revolutionary period. The failure of the Revolution had brought with it a feeling that the moment had come for a more realistic approach to problems and the pursuit of the more concrete goals of scientific and technological progress. It was an atmosphere propitious for the introduction of the philosophy of positivism. In the 1870s a debate was waged in newspapers, magazines and professional academies as to whether positivist philosophy, with its emphasis on conformity with ascertained facts as the sole yardstick of truth and its claim to apply the scientific method to all areas of life, was a more suitable basis for progress than the idealist metaphysics of Krausism which had inspired the reforms of the revolutionary period. The philosophical debate was paralleled by an aesthetic debate between Idealism and Realism, the latter being widely regarded as the application of positivist principles to art. Put simply, literary Idealism favoured the portrayal of man and society as they ought to be, Realism as they were. Whereas Idealism took as its starting point the preconceived idea and placed great value on the imagination, Realism adopted a method based on the observation of material reality.[5]

Marianela is no less rooted in the ideological conflicts of the late 1870s than *Doña Perfecta*, *Gloria*, or *La familia de León Roch*. There is undoubtedly a change in tone and also of focus from political and religious questions to philosophical and social themes but all these issues are interrelated and it is important, as Peter Goldman points out, not to oversimplify and separate or weigh them against each other (*19*, p. 16, note 32). Galdós's fundamental concern was with the problems involved in regenerating a backward society and how he as a novelist could best contribute to this regeneration. This preoccupation with progress not only links *Marianela* to the other three novels but also connects the questions relating to philosophy, scientific and industrial advance, social reform and aesthetics which he raises in the novel.

Before discussing these questions in detail, I wish to comment briefly on the two approaches which have dominated criticism on *Marianela*: the search for sources and the elaboration of symbolical interpretations. Much of the critical controversy over the novel is linked to rival claims regarding Galdós's sources which have commonly been assumed to hold the key to the meaning of the novel. Sources have been found in philosophy, literature, historical reality and the author's own life; they include Comte, Plato, Taine, Diderot, Goethe, Ayguals de Izco, Castiglione, San Juan de la Cruz, Dante, Calderón, the picaresque novel, Victor Hugo, Eugène Sue, Charles Nodier, Wilkie Collins, the parliamentary speeches of Emilio Castelar, and Galdós's frustrated love for his cousin Sisita. The sheer number and variety of sources which have been proposed indicates the extreme difficulty of identifying them with any accuracy. Often the similarities with *Marianela* are exceedingly slight: a casual

[5]For both the philosophical and the literary debate see Nuñez Ruiz (*6*); see also Gifford Davis, 'The Spanish Debate over Idealism and Realism before the Impact of Zola's Naturalism', *PMLA*, 84 (1969), 1649-56; Mariano López, 'Los escritores de la Restauración y las polémicas literarias del siglo XIX en España, *Bulletin Hispanique*, 81 (1979), 51-73.

similarity of metaphor, a commonplace idea, blind heroes or heroines, exploited orphans, unhappy love affairs, suicides and even
keen-witted dogs: the presence of any one of these in a work has
been considered as sufficient proof that Galdós drew on it. Even
where the evidence is more substantial, as in the case of Goethe's
Wilhelm Meister for example, it seems more likely, as Montesinos
suggests (*24*, p. 238), that this was a 'sugestión' rather than a source.
Obviously Galdós found inspiration in what he read just as he found
inspiration in the real world, but to hypothesize exactly how the
different elements were put together is a fruitless exercise.

Even more problematic is the attempt to discover the supposed
symbolical significance of the novel by relating it to a specific source
or sources. *Marianela* is undeniably a novel which invites interpretation on an abstract level: setting, characters, plot, dialogue and
imagery, as we shall see, all constantly encourage the reader to find
in them a significance which goes beyond that of a simple story of
individual relationships. It is not surprising, therefore, that symbolical interpretations abound; the following summary does not pretend
to be exhaustive. For example, it has been suggested that Galdós
wished to illustrate how Spain or the Spanish people (Pablo), en-
lightened by science, progress, education (Teodoro), should turn
away from primitive and underdeveloped faith, superstition, ignorance (Nela) to modern religion (Florentina) (*44, 46*); to expose the
deficiencies of the attitude of Spain (Florentina) to her colonies
(Marianela) (*57*); to illustrate August Comte's law of the three stages
of human evolution, the theological (Nela), the metaphysical (Pablo)
and the positivistic (Teodoro) with Florentina representing Comte's
concept of the Virgin (*12*); to illustrate Pablo's spiritual progress in
Platonic terms from a pre-rational state (Nela), through idealistic
rationalism (Teodoro) towards reality, reason and absolute beauty
(Florentina) (*52*). Further refinements or modifications are offered
by critics who argue for different correspondences or propose
additional sources. Thus, for example, Pattison (*50*) adds equivalences from Goethe's *Wilhelm Meister* to the Comtian symbolism, whereas Marie Wellington (*53*) suggests different Comtian
equivalences; Dendle (*40*) accepts Ruiz's Platonic symbolism but
interprets it differently and adds equivalences from Ayguals de
Izco's *La belleza del alma*. Interpretations of this kind are generally

characterized by the positing of detailed and precise correspondences between characters and events in the novel and elements in the
supposed source text. They are based on the assumption that the
text has a single, coherently expressed meaning which is identifiable
with authorial intention and can be discovered by the critic. This
presupposition would be rejected by most modern critical theorists,
and the very fact that *Marianela* has lent itself to such a wide range
of different and often contradictory interpretations should at least
make us suspicious of it. Galdós's own concept of the novel at this
stage was, moreover, antithetical to such a notion: commenting on
Gloria in a letter to Pereda of 10 March 1877, that is shortly before
embarking on *Marianela*, he says 'yo no he querido probar en dicha
novela ninguna tesis filosófica ni religiosa, porque para eso no se
escriben novelas'.[6] There is symbolical intention in Galdós's fiction,
but rather than one rigid and fixed meaning as in allegory, there is a
range of possible meanings. There is no reason to believe that his
views on symbolism changed between 1878 and 1902 when in the
prologue to his play, *Alma y Vida*, he wrote:

> Y el simbolismo no sería bello si fuese claro, con solución
> descifrable mecánicamente como la de las charadas. Déjenle,
> pues, su vaguedad de ensueño y no le busquen la derivación
> lógica ni la moraleja del cuento de niños. Si tal tuviera y se nos
> presentara sus figuras y accidentes ajustados a clave, perdería
> todo su encanto, privando a los que lo escuchan o contemplan
> del íntimo goce de la interpretación personal. (p. 903)

[6]Carmen Bravo Villasante, 'Veintiocho cartas de Galdós a Pereda', p. 18.

2 *Progress*

The doctrine of progress which had steadily been gaining adherents since the Renaissance acquired even greater authority in the nineteenth century with the spectacular advances in science and technology.[7] To what extent Galdós shared the widespread optimism that the progress of science must mean the progress of civilization is a much-debated question: whereas some see *Marianela* as a profession of positivist faith in the progress of humanity through science (*12*; *50*), others suggest it shows Galdós to be at best dubious about the advantages of a positivistic outlook and the achievements of science (*16*; *37*; *42*; *53*).

Science and Philosophy

In the Spain of the 1870s positivism, as we have seen, began to supersede Krausism as the philosophy which could provide the most solid foundations for progress. Both positivists and Krausists had a great respect for science and the methods of scientific investigation but, whereas positivists believed that progress depended primarily on the application of the scientific method to all areas of life, Krausists gave equal if not greater importance to ethics and metaphysics and believed that reason was the chief motor of social and political change. Positivists argued that only a knowledge of facts was possible and that observation and experience were the only legitimate methods of acquiring knowledge. The Krausists, on the other hand, argued that matters of fact and experience should be referred to reasoning and claimed that through reason and metaphysical speculation man could understand areas of life that could not be verified by observation. Undoubtedly, it was the ethical and social implications of positivism which caused most concern: how could a philosophy which had limited itself to explaining material reality and relegated everything else to the unknowable realm of theology and

[7]See Sidney Pollard, *The Idea of Progress: History and Society* (Harmondsworth: Penguin, 1971), and Walter E. Houghton, *The Victorian Mind, 1830-1870* (New Haven: Yale University Press, 1957), Chapter 2.

metaphysics provide a foundation for ethics? This was the central issue of a series of debates held in 1875-76 in the Sección de Ciencias Morales y Políticas of the Ateneo of Madrid in which metaphysical idealists — Krausists, Hegelians and eclectics — found themselves on the defensive against the combined forces of positivists and neo-Kantians.[8] Although there is no doubt that Galdós draws on both Comtian positivism (*12*; *50*; *51*; *53*) and Platonic idealism (*40*; *52*) for some of the philosophical material in *Marianela*, it seems probable that these debates in the Ateneo provided the immediate stimulus for the writing of the novel: Galdós was personally acquainted with several of the participants and, as a member of the Ateneo, he may even have attended some sessions himself. The emphasis on the practical implications of positivism undoubtedly appealed to him for, as Alas tells us, Galdós's interest in philosophy was 'en su aplicación a la conducta de los hombres' and not in 'la especulación por la especulación' (*31*, p. 35). *Marianela* was his own contribution to the contemporary debate on the relative validity of idealist and materialist interpretations of reality and their ethical and social implications.

The controversy over the philosophical message of the novel, whether the focus is on positivism or Platonism, has centred on whether the consequences of Pablo's transition from blindness to sight — his changed concept of reality and the transference of his affections from Nela to Florentina — should be seen as positive or negative: a tribute to science and the positivist method or a tragic sacrifice of inner vision and eternal spiritual values to the transitory and material; an evolution, like that of Plato's cave dwellers, from

[8]The neo-Kantians accepted the methods of positivism and the separation between the knowable and the unknowable but argued that the latter was accessible to feeling and faith. The title of the debates was: 'El actual movimiento de las ciencias naturales y filosóficas en sentido positivista, ¿constituye un grave peligro para los grandes principios morales, sociales y religiosos en que descansan la civilización?' See the reports in the *Revista Contemporánea* by Manuel de la Revilla: 1 (1875-76), 121-28, 246-47, 523-26; 2 (1876), 383-86; 3 (1876), 125-27; by Rafael Montoro, 2 (1876), 121-30 and by Gumersindo de Azcárate, 3 (1876), 350-67, 4 (1876), 230-50 and 465-99. The last was reprinted as 'El positivismo y la civilización' in Azcárate's *Estudios filosóficos y políticos* (Madrid. Imp. de Manuel M. de los Ríos, 1877), pp.1-125. For the importance of science in Krausist ideology see Yvonne Turin, '1868. Révolution scientifique: étude idéologique du mouvement révolutionnaire espagnol', *Revue Historique*, 258 (1977), 353-62. See also *6*, *17*, and *50*.

ignorance to true knowledge (*52*), or an abandonment of 'rationally perceived universal truths in favour of, in Platonic terms, the slavery of the sensual and contingent' (*40*, p. 9).

Pablo's concept of reality while he is blind is fundamentally based on rationalist metaphysics. That is, he believes that reasoning is a reliable source of knowledge. Deprived of all direct contact with the visible world, his knowledge comes principally from books and meditation. He has an 'entendimiento de primer orden', fostered by his father who has paid great attention 'a su instrucción y a su educación cristiana' (V, 719). He enjoys philosophical speculation and his favourite books are those which deal with 'ideas sobre las causas y los efectos. Sobre el por qué de lo que pensamos y el modo cómo lo pensamos, y enseñan la esencia de todas las cosas' (VII, 723). He refers the evidence of his senses to his reason, as for example when he deduces that a piece of limestone must be beautiful because it is pleasing to his touch (II, 708). He believes that the divine can be rationally apprehended: 'si Dios no nos ha dado alas', he asserts, 'en cambio nos ha dado el pensamiento, que vuela más que todos los pájaros, porque llega hasta el mismo Dios' (VII, 723). He is convinced that although ignorant of the visible world, he has access to an internal or spiritual truth: 'no veo lo de fuera, pero veo lo de dentro, y todas las maravillas de tu alma se me han revelado desde que eres mi lazarillo' (VI, 722), he tells Nela. His faith in the validity of his own vision is such that he distrusts knowledge acquired by observation and affirms: 'el don de la vista puede causar grandes extravíos ..., aparta a los hombres de la verdad absoluta' (VII, 725).

Pablo's idealist vision of the world is revealed most clearly in his concept of beauty. Influenced by a work in which beauty is defined as 'el resplandor de la bondad y de la verdad', he believes that there is an absolute, ideal beauty, 'una belleza que no se ve ni se toca, ni se percibe con ningún sentido [...] una sola belleza, y que ésa había de servir para todo' (VII, 724). Pablo thus has a Platonic concept of a single, transcendental form of beauty, not seen with the eyes but grasped conceptually by the mind alone, a beauty necessarily related to moral and spiritual qualities.[9] This *a priori* concept of beauty

[9]For Platonic concepts in *Marianela* see *40* and *52*; for a general study see Gustavo Correa, 'Galdós y el platonismo', *AG*, 7 (1972), 3-17. Marie Wellington (*54*) suggests Diderot's *Traité du beau* as the source for the discussions on beauty.

leads him to the conviction — for which, he claims, 'no me hacen falta los ojos' — that Nela must be 'la belleza más acabada que puede imaginarse'. If this were not the case, he argues, 'faltaría la lógica de las bellezas, y eso no puede ser' (VII, 724). Pablo's last appearance before he gains his sight is in Chapter XV where, dismissing Nela's assertion that Florentina is as beautiful as the Virgin, he once again affirms the superiority of his inner vision: 'no puede ser tan hermosa como dices . . . ¿Crees que yo, sin ojos, no comprendo dónde está la hermosura y dónde no?' (XV, 749). Nevertheless, his anxious questions which conclude the chapter hint at the precariousness of his idealist vision of the world: '¿De qué modo se retrata el alma en las caras? Si la luz no sirve para enseñarnos lo real de nuestro pensamiento, ¿para qué sirve? Lo que es y lo que se siente, ¿no son como el calor y el fuego? ¿Pueden separarse? ¿Puedes dejar de ser tú para mí el más hermoso, el más amado de todos los seres de la Tierra, cuando yo me hago dueño de los dominios de la forma?' (XV, 750).

Pablo's initial view of reality based only on reason and imagination is clearly defective, His reason, Don Francisco argues, has been over-stimulated and has developed 'una cantidad de ideas superiores a la capacidad del cerebro de un hombre que no ve'. Pablo has attempted to compensate for his lack of sight with the 'atrevidas creaciones' of his imagination but this is merely 'un Hércules atado con cadenas dentro de un calabozo'. Without sight, don Francisco concludes, his 'asombroso espíritu de indagación' is merely a 'valiente pájaro con las alas rotas'. Teodoro says of Pablo, 'en él todo es idealismo, un idealismo grandioso, enormemente bello [...] no conoce la realidad . . . ; vive la vida interior, la vida de la ilusión pura'. Teodoro suspects that by giving Pablo sight he may convert him 'de ángel en hombre' but affirms that the duty of science is to make him a man: 'traigámosle del mundo de las ilusiones a la esfera de la realidad y entonces sus ideas serán exactas, tendrá el don de apreciar en su verdadero valor todas las cosas', a conviction echoed by don Francisco (XI, 737).

After the successful operation Pablo's new knowledge of material reality leads him to reject his earlier idealist concept of beauty for one based on form unrelated to moral qualities: 'el vigoroso entendimiento del joven propendía siempre a distinguir la fealdad de la

hermosura. Distinguía estas dos ideas en absoluto sin que influyera
nada en él ni la idea de utilidad, ni aún la de bondad' (XX, 764). The
beautiful Florentina now represents for him 'un tipo perfecto de
hermosura' and, scorning his 'ridícula vanidad de ciego', his 'necio
empeño de apreciar sin vista el aspecto de las cosas', he exclaims
' ¡La realidad! El que no la posee es un idiota' (XX, 765). Thus, his
earlier idealist interpretation of the world, which equated reality
with the spiritual, gives way to a materialist interpretation which
equates reality with the visible world: observation not reason is now
his guide to reality.

What are the implications of this rejection of metaphysical idealism in favour of the authority of experience? The patterns of imagery which Galdós uses to structure his story, especially those of sight
and blindness, light and darkness, and those connected with the New
World, have been invoked to support both positive (*48*; *52*) and
negative (*37*; *39*; *40*) interpretations of Pablo's evolution. Does
Pablo evolve from ignorance, symbolized by his blindness and the
'perpetuas tinieblas' in which he lives, to knowledge, symbolized by
his sight and the light, or has the physical light blinded him to spiritual reality and extinguished the 'portentosa luz interior' (V, 719)
which he previously enjoyed? Has he progressed from the Dantesque
hell of the mines of the early chapters to the heavenly light of revelation of the final chapters, or is his revelation, as Krebs suggests, an
ironic reversal of that of his namesake St Paul who was converted to
Christianity after being blinded by a supernatural light (*43*,
pp. 37-38)? Do the images of the New World used to describe
Pablo's discovery of the visible world (Chapter XX, 765, XXI, 771,
772) have the same positive and optimistic connotations which they
seem to have when used to describe Teodoro's achievements (XI,
736), or are they intended to remind us, as Dendle suggests (*39*,
pp. 337-38), of the less attractive elements which accompanied the
discovery of the New World, especially the *conquistadores'* lust for
gold?

Although the ambiguity of the images discourages a simple interpretation of Pablo's evolution as either wholly negative or wholly
positive, most of the evidence seems to suggest that by impetuously
identifying the real with the visible world he has, rather than passing
from ignorance to knowledge, from illusion to reality, as some claim

(*12*; *46*; *50*; *52*), merely exchanged one defective vision of the world for another (*16*; *24*; *40*; *42*; *51*; *53*). His vision, as Montesinos (*24*, I, pp. 238-39) suggests, is pagan rather than positivist, closer to Nela's than to Teodoro's: like her, he worships physical beauty, having discovered through Florentina the New World 'del amor por la forma' (XXI, 772). Moreover, Pablo's knowledge of material reality seems to have blinded him to spiritual realities he was previously able to perceive. By accepting the conventional view of Nela as a 'monstruo' (XXI, 771), he seems to have fallen into the snare against which he warned so often when he was blind: the deceptiveness of appearances. As the narrator remarks, 'podría decirse de él, como de muchos que nunca fueron ciegos de los ojos, que sólo veía lo que tenía delante' (XXI, 770).

The argument that Pablo's rejection of Nela in favour of Florentina and Nela's death represent a necessary evolution from an inferior to a superior stage fails to convince whether it is framed in positivist terms (*12*) as humanity freed from the imagination and brought to reality by Science, or in Platonic terms (*52*) as the transition from a pre-rational to a rational state. If anything, his callous treatment of Nela suggests that Galdós shared the commonplace fears that the materialist concept of reality was a threat to ethics. The intense pathos of the death scene and Teodoro's anguish at his powerlessness to save Nela indicate more than a passing regret at the inevitable demise of the values she represents. Florentina is of course physically more beautiful than Nela and she enjoys the benefits of an intellectual and religious education, but there is no suggestion that she is inherently superior spiritually or morally to Nela (see Chapter 3). Moreover, although Nela's view of reality, which is based on the senses, feeling and imagination, is clearly defective the novel depends for its effect largely on our recognition of the beauty of her soul and its potential for development, a potential analogous to that of Pablo for physical sight: Teodoro says that characters like Nela 'viven ciegos del espíritu, como Pablo Penáguilas ha vivido ciego del cuerpo teniendo vista' (XXI, 769). Teodoro hopes to rescue Nela from intellectual and spiritual darkness by bringing her the light of instruction and Christian teaching, just as he rescued Pablo from physical darkness by restoring his sight. He wants to enable her to discover the New World of her soul (XIX, 762), the world of the spirit which for her is as yet 'una región confusa, una tierra apenas descubierta, de la cual no se tiene sino noticias vagas por algún viajero náufrago' (XXI, 769), just as he has enabled Pablo to discover the New World of light and form (XX). This analogy, which is maintained by the patterns of imagery of light and darkness and of the New World, suggests that if Galdós has a philosophical message, it is that the material and the spiritual world are of equal importance and that there is a need to find a balance between the two. A closer examination of the role of Teodoro provides further evidence for this conclusion.

Teodoro, a successful and famous ophthalmic surgeon, passionately committed to his own discipline, whose motto is 'adelante siempre adelante', seems to be an obvious representative of science and positivist method in the service of progress (*12*; *50*). Doctors in the nineteenth century enjoyed considerable prestige; in Spain they not only formed the vanguard of scientific progress but were also actively involved in social reforms — education, treatment of the insane and penal reform. Teodoro, like most of Galdós's doctors, is characterized not only by his devotion to science but by his humanitarian concerns and, as Marie Wellington (*53*) points out, he does not reject reason, observation, or God.[10] If anything, he seems to represent a balance between the material and the spiritual. Furthermore, his experiences lead him to question his own faith in science — a faith which in any event is always more restrained and cautious than that of Pepe Rey, the protagonist of *Doña Perfecta* (see *48*).

Initially, as we have seen, he is confident that a proper appreciation of reality depends upon observation and that his duty as a scientist is, therefore, to give Pablo his sight even if this means destroying his illusions. The decision to go ahead, made only after Teodoro has explained to don Francisco the dangers of the operation, is endorsed by the narrator: 'era preciso hacer frente a los más grandes misterios de la vida, interrogarlos y explorar las causas que

[10]For Galdós's interest in medicine and admiration and respect for doctors see Walter Rubin, 'Galdós y la medicina', *Atlántida,* 8 (1970), 68-80; Luis S. Granjel, 'Personajes médicos de Galdós', *CHA*, nos 250-52 (1970-71), 656-63; and Florencio L. Pérez Bautista, *Sociedad y medicina en la novela realista española*, Cuadernos de Historia de la Medicina Española, Monografías, 27 (Salamanca: Ediciones del Instituto de la Medicina Española, 1974). Ophthalmology developed as a specialist discipline in the last decadesof the nineteenth century: see Luis Granjel, *Historia de la oftalmología española* (Salamanca: Gráf. Cervantes, 1964), pp.85-109.

impedían a los ojos de un hombre el conocimiento de la realidad visible.' Teodoro is described as 'intrépido y sereno' and the operation as an 'audaz expedición por el interior de un mundo microscópico, empresa no menos colosal que medir la distancia de los astros en las infinitudes del espacio' (XVI, 750). Teodoro, however, is aware that medical knowledge can only go so far and awaits with equanimity the results of the operation: 'la ciencia había hecho todo lo que sabía. Era un simulacro de la creación, como otros muchos que son gloria y orgullo del siglo XIX. En presencia de tanta audacia, La Naturaleza, que no permite sean sorprendidos sus secretos, continuaba muda y reservada' (XVI, 750; cf. XI, 739). Teodoro guides Pablo's entry into the visible world with scientific curiosity and prudent concern. However, he comes to realize that his scientific success has brought human distress: 'la realidad ha sido para él nueva vida; para ella ha sido dolor y asfixia, la humillación, la tristeza, el desaire, el dolor . . . , ¡la muerte!' (XXI, 773). Teodoro's sense of helplessness at Nela's final collapse and death brings home to him with full force the limitations of science. He soon abandons medical remedies which only cruelly prolong her life, postponing the remedy sent by God – death. He realizes that the true cause of her rapid decline is not physical – a 'meningitis fulminante' – but psychological and that he, a doctor 'de los ojos no de las pasiones' (XXI, 772), a mere 'carpintero de los ojos' (XXI, 773), is impotent to save her. 'Es que no sabemos más que fenómenos superficiales', he observes as he contemplates the dying Nela – 'aquel libro humano de caracteres oscuros, en los cuales la vista científica no podía descifrar la leyenda misteriosa de la muerte y la vida' (XXI, 773). There is no trace of the confident optimism usually associated with the positivist outlook in this scene. On the contrary, Teodoro's comments are an explicit rejection of the positivist contention that mind was merely an extension of matter and that intellectual, moral and affective phenomena might ultimately be explainable by a study of the nervous system. Indeed, Leopoldo Alas, relating *Marianela* to the contemporary debates on the reality of the spirit, asserted that Galdós had succeeded where orators in academic debates had failed, in arousing 'en el lector atento el sentimiento y el sentido de la trascendencia del espíritu, de su realidad inmediata' (*31*, pp. 73-74).[11]

The fact that the novel ends by challenging aspects of the positivistic outlook and emphasizing the limitations rather than the achievements of science does not mean that Galdós rejected either positivism or science, but merely that he did not see them as panaceas. The narrator's endorsement of Teodoro's decision to operate, and the enthusiastic, detailed, technical descriptions of this miracle of modern science, suggest that Galdós had a genuine pride in the scientific achievements of his age. Moreover, there is no doubt that he was influenced by positivist ideas and attached importance to observation and experience as means of acquiring knowledge, but his awareness of the complexity of life prevented him from embracing wholeheartedly such a narrowly empirical philosophy (*20*, p. 120; *22*, p. 16, note 21).[12]

Science and Industry

Science in the nineteenth century captured the public imagination and inspired confidence above all for its contributions to technology and industry. Advances in these fields were viewed as evidence of man's ability to conquer nature and harness her material resources to his own needs: whereas primitive man, argued Gumersindo de Azcárate, had been 'anonadado bajo el imperio incontrastable de las

[11] In his summary of the debates on the question '¿Puede y debe considerarse la vida de los seres organizados como transformación de la fuerza universal?', held in the session 1875-76 by the Sección de Ciencias Naturales of the Ateneo de Madrid, Manuel de la Revilla emphasized that neither the experimental method of positivist science nor the spiritualist currents had been able to 'esclarecer los misteriosos problemas que la vida encierra, principalmente en su aspecto psíquico'. The debates had shown, he continued, the need to recognize the existence of something we call 'espíritu, y acerca de cuyo origen y naturaleza nada sabemos, ni en la esfera científica podemos saber': 'Revista crítica', *RC*, 2 (1876), 505-07 (pp. 505-06). Galdós satirized the materialist concept of the soul in an early article: 'Manicomio social: Jaula Segunda. —El filósofo materialista', *La Nación* (15 March 1868), reproduced in William H. Shoemaker, *Los artículos de Galdós en 'La Nación': 1865-1866, 1868* (Madrid: Insula, 1972), pp. 458-61.

[12] The use of 'positivismo' to denote a philosophical system that bases knowledge on perception should not be confused with its more general use to denote a pragmatic and materialistic attitude. Galdós uses it in the latter sense in his attack on 'el positivismo de las aldeas' in chapter IV.

fuerzas naturales', for contemporary man the forces of nature were 'dóciles instrumentos ... de que se sirve para su bien'.[13] The achievements in engineering – the Suez Canal was built between 1856 and 1869 – were particularly remarkable and it is no coincidence that Galdós chose engineers as protagonists of *Doña Perfecta* and *La familia de León Roch*, novels which dramatize the conflict between progress and reaction. In *Marianela* Carlos Golfín, the engineer, plays only a subsidiary role but the world of technology and industry, which is something of an abstraction in the other two novels, comes alive through the descriptions of the mines. It was an appropriate choice: the subsoil had been disentailed (formerly the property of the State, it had been put up for public sale) after the Revolution of 1868, and capital, both Spanish and foreign, flowed into the mining industry, converting it into a new 'El Dorado' and bringing Spain into the world capitalist system.[14] For some (*11*; *12*; *48*; *50*) Galdós's portrayal of the industrial world is primarily positive, a tribute to man's technological achievements and their material consequences: for others it reveals a distrustful (*39*) or even a downright hostile attitude (*37*).

We first see the mines from the perspective of Teodoro who describes them in a series of similes which certainly suggest that Galdós was sensitive to the negative effects of industrialization on the landscape. In the half-light the rocks of the zone known as 'la Terrible', now no longer mined, seem like 'figuras colosales, hombres disformes, monstruos volcados y patas arriba'; it is as if they had been caught at the moment of death: 'parecía la petrificación de una orgía de gigantescos demonios', and in this terrifying silence 'mil voces y aullidos habían quedado también hechos piedra, y piedra eran desde siglos de siglos' (II, 705). For Teodoro it is a 'pesadilla',

---

[13]'El positivismo y la civilización', *Estudios filosóficos y políticos*, p.56. In 1872 Galdós had planned to report on 'las grandes conquistas del genio contemporáneo, en el comercio y en la industria' in his column in the fortnightly *La Ilustración de Madrid* but in the event produced nothing on the topic: Benito Pérez Galdós, *Crónica de la quincena*, William H. Shoemaker (Princeton: University Press, 1948), p. 28.

[14]See Nicolás Sánchez Albornoz, *España hace un siglo: una economía dual* (Madrid: Alianza, 1977), pp. 140-42, and Jordi Nadal, *El fracaso de la revolución industrial en España, 1814-1913*, 3rd printing (Barcelona: Ariel, 1979), chapter 4. The mines of Reocín on which Galdós based those of Socartes were owned at this period by the Real Compañía Asturiana (*8*, p.253; see also pp. 31-32).

an 'espectáculo asombroso', like a brain attacked by a violent head-
ache (II, 705-06). He compares a gallery he and Pablo pass through
to an oesophagus and themselves to 'pobres bichos' who have fallen
into the stomach of an insectivore (II, 706). They emerge from the
gallery into the even more remarkable scene presented by the section
known as 'El Barco' because of its resemblance to the inside of a
wrecked ship. Teodoro imagines he can see 'mil despojos de cosas
náuticas, cadáveres medio devorados por los peces, momias,
esqueletos, todo muerto, dormido, semidescompuesto y profun-
damente tranquilo, cual si por mucho tiempo morara en la inmensa
sepultura del mar' (II, 707). The next part of their route reminds
him of 'los pensamientos del hombre perverso. Aquí se representa la
intuición del malo cuando penetra en su conciencia para verse en
toda su fealdad' (II, 707). When he finally arrives at the furnaces he
comments: 'más hermoso es esto para verlo una vez que para vivir
aquí' (III, 712). This predominantly negative impression is reinforced by the fact that the opening chapters, as many critics have
pointed out, deliberately echo Dante's *Inferno* with Pablo-Virgil
leading Teodoro-Dante through hell — the mines.

It must be noted, however, that not all is negative: the general
view is that 'la Terrible' presents 'un golpe de vista sublime' (II, 705)
and Teodoro himself recognizes that the mines have a certain beauty
(III, 712). Moreover, we must remember that these descriptions are
presented from Teodoro's subjective point of view: later, la Terrible,
seen in the daytime and described in a series of picturesque comparisons by Florentina who finds it 'muy bonito', is far less threaten-
ing:

> Aquella piedra grande que está en medio tiene su gran boca,
> ¿no la ves, Nela?, y en la boca tiene un palillo de dientes; es
> una planta que ha nacido sola. Parece que se ríe mirándonos,
> porque también tiene ojos; y más allá hay una con joroba, y
> otra que fuma en pipa, y dos que se están tirando de los pelos,
> y una que bosteza, y otra que duerme la mona, y otra que está
> boca abajo, sosteniendo con los pies una catedral, y otra que
> empieza en guitarra y acaba en cabeza de perro, con una
> cafetera por gorro. (XV, 748)

The purpose of this amusing description seems to be less to suggest 'the destructive process of mineral exploitation and its consequent dereliction' as Bly (*37*, p.53) suggests, than to alert us to the way in which visible reality is transformed through the power of the imagination. The mines are thus drawn into the theme of the deceptiveness of appearances: Pablo tells Florentina 'todo eso que dices, primita[...] me prueba que con los ojos se ven muchos disparates, lo cual indica que ése órgano tan precioso sirve a veces para presentar las cosas desfiguradas, cambiando los objetos de su natural forma en otra postiza y fingida' (XV, 748). For Pablo, Teodoro's monsters and Florentina's giants are merely 'bloques de piedra que llaman cretácea y de arcilla ferruginosa endurecida que han quedado después de sacado el mineral' (II, 705); 'rocas cretáceas y masas de tierra caliza, embadurnadas con óxido de hierro' (XV, 748). The deliberate contrast between the subjective, imaginative descriptions of the sighted and the factual, scientific descriptions provided by the blind Pablo, and the irony that it is the latter who guides the lost Teodoro through the mines, ought perhaps to warn us not to attach too much weight to the apparently negative associations of the early descriptions of the mines.

Unlike the personal visions of the mines ascribed implicitly or explicitly to Teodoro and Florentina, the description at the beginning of chapter V is unascribed. For Bly (*37*, p. 52) this is the climax of Galdós's protest at the unnatural, destructive character of the mine; for Casalduero (*28*, p.88, note 3) an 'espléndido canto épico a la industria'. The description is open to both interpretations but the prevailing impression, I believe, is less one of sorrow at the dehumanization of the workers than of wonder at the spectacular drama of industrialization: the vast number of workers, the ceaseless activity of machines and men, even the infernal noise. There is undeniably terror in the wonder but the comparisons Galdós employs suggest admiration rather than condemnation: 'el martillo, dando porrazos uniformes creaba formas nuevas tan duras como las geológicas, que son obra laboriosa de los siglos. Se parecen mucho, sí, las obras de la fuerza a las de la paciencia' (V, 717); the glowing metal extracted from the furnaces is an 'extraña escultura' which has 'por genio el fuego y por cincel el martillo'; the miners are 'los escultores de aquellas caprichosas e ingentes figuras que permanecían en pie, atentas, con gravedad silenciosa, a la invasión del hombre en las misteriosas esferas geológicas' (V, 717). The description culminates with a tribute to 'el silicato de zinc, esa plata de Europa que no por ser la materia de que se hacen las cacerolas deja de ser grandiosa fuente de bienestar y civilización. Sobre ella ha alzado Bélgica el estandarte de su grandeza moral y política. ¡Oh! La hoja de lata tiene también su epopeya' (V, 718). The tribute is taken at face value by Casalduero (*28*, p. 90, note 9) and Pattison (*50*, p. 132) but as ironic by Bly (*37*, p. 51), who argues that 'esa plata de Europa' suggests a parallel with plundering of South America by the Spanish *conquistadores* and implies that in this case too the consequences will be material and moral ruin. Beyrie's view that Galdós's perspective is one of strict liberal orthodoxy (*11*, II, p. 288) seems, however, more probable since we know from external evidence that he welcomed foreign investment in Spanish industry.[15]

Galdós's treatment of the social question, which will be studied in detail in Chapter 3, also suggests that he did not intend to make a vigorous attack on industrial development. Although he was clearly concerned about the possible physical and moral effects of industrialization on the workers, he does not provide detailed descriptions of their conditions nor does he choose as the representative of industrialization a figure such as Dicken's Josiah Bounderby of *Hard Times* or Mrs Gaskell's Thornton of *North and South* — characters who incarnate the aggressive money-making and power-seeking ideal which was the driving force of the industrial revolution. His representative is the engineer, Carlos, who is described as 'muy pacífico, estudioso, esclavo de su deber, apasionado por la Minerología y la Metalurgía' (IX, 730). Despite Teodoro's humorous explanation of the etymology of their surname — '*Gold*, oro; *to find*, hallar . . . Es, como si dijéramos, buscador de oro . . . He aquí que mientras mi

---

[15]Galdós wrote in *Las Cortes* (29 April 1869): 'Pero también dijo el Sr. Ortiz de Zárate (¡que hombre!) que *aquí no había extranjeros ni necesitábamos de los extranjeros, los cuales únicamente venían a poner alguna fonda o a hacer comercio menudo* . . . ¿Quién explota las minas de Llinares? ¿Quién riega los campos de Guadalajara? ¿Quién fabrica las porcelanas de Sevilla? ¿Quién forja los hierros de Málaga? ¿Quién ha trazado y construido aquí los primeros ferro carriles [sic]?'; quoted by Beyrie (*11*, III, p. 165, note 78). In *Miau* (1888) Galdós satirizes the civil servant Pantoja for his narrow-minded distrust of foreign investment.

hermano lo busca en las entrañas de la tierra, yo lo busco en el interior maravilloso de ese universo en abreviatura que se llama el ojo humano' (IX, 730) — there is no suggestion that Carlos's moral life has been blunted by the pursuit of wealth; the most he could be charged with is showing more devotion to his work than to his wife and of having done little for Nela. Carlos's duties seem to be scientific rather than managerial and apart from a brief reference to the hours spent in the laboratory (IX, 729) we see neither him nor the 'jefe del taller de maquinaria', the Englishman, Ulises Bull, at work.

It is don Manuel Penáguilas who most obviously incarnates the moral philistinism associated with the devotees of material progress and, as far as we know, he has no connection with the industrial world. His physical appearance suggests the self-satisfied bourgeois who likes to advertise his wealth in his very person: 'parecía echar de sí rayos de satisfacción como el sol los echa de luz; pequeño de piernas, un poco largo de nariz, y magnificado con varios objetos decorativos, entre los cuales descollaba una gran cadena de reloj y un fino sombrero de fieltro de alas anchas' (XIV, 746). He clearly identifies progress with material advancement and when Florentina compares the beautiful countryside of Aldeacorba with the 'triste tierra de Campo' where they live, he comments: '¡Oh! No hables mal de Santa Irene de Campo, una villa ilustrada, donde se encuentran hoy muchas comodidades y una sociedad distinguida. También han llegado allí los adelantos de la civilización . . . , de la civilización' (XIV, 746). His admiration for material progress goes hand in hand with a petty social snobbery and a certain lack of moral delicacy but all in all the portrait is gently ironical rather than satirical.

Against the modern industrial world of the mines of Socartes Galdós sets the traditional rural world of Aldeacorba whose chief representative is don Francisco Penáguilas. His portrait contains nothing to suggest that Galdós believed this world and those who belonged to it to be inherently superior to the world of industrialization. His wealth has been largely inherited — 'heredó regular hacienda y en la época de nuestra historia acababa de heredar otra mayor' (V, 719) — and he lacks the energy and drive of the two self-made professional men who represent the modern world of science and technology. His occupations are not demanding — writing a letter to his brother, milking a cow, pruning a tree, seeing if a chicken has laid an egg. Though he is not portrayed as being actively engaged in the pursuit of wealth, his concerns are largely material: he wants his son to have sight so he can enjoy 'las delicias honradas de la buena posición', admire the fat cattle, the laden fruit trees, pay his workers and forecast the weather from the skies, and make a good marriage which will permit the transfer of property from one generation to the next (XI, 738).[16] The narrator, it is true, stresses his positive characteristics: 'era un hombre más que bueno, era inmejorable, superiormente discreto, bondadoso, afable, honrado y magnánimo, no falta de instrucción. Nadie le aborreció jamás; era el más respetado de todos los propietarios ricos del país y más de una cuestión se arregló por la mediación, siempre inteligente, del *señor de Aldeacorba de Suso*' (V, 719). Nevertheless, wrapped up in his own concerns, he lacks the social sensibility of Teodoro.

The description of don Francisco's house, which immediately follows that of the mines in chapter V, clearly links it to the feudal world of the past: it is a 'primorosa vivienda infanzona' with an 'ancho escudo'. In contrast to the hustle and bustle of the mines, the house 'respiraba paz, bienestar y una conciencia tranquila' (V, 718). It has a beautiful orchard and a meadow where the cows graze. The next three chapters present the surrounding countryside — the trees, flowers, lanes, hills, streams and distant sea — which provides a most appropriate backcloth for the idyll between Pablo and Marianela. It is undoubtedly magnificent: 'era un paisaje cuya contemplación revelaba al alma sus excelsas relaciones con lo infinito' (VII, 723). This luxuriant countryside is evoked again in chapter XIV as a background to Nela's vision of Florentina as the Virgin Mary. Nevertheless, just as the mines have their own peculiar magnificence, so the countryside is not without its sombre aspects: for Pablo la Trascava, the bottomless crevice down which Nela's mother threw herself and where Nela herself attempts to commit suicide, is 'horrenda', a place which inspires terror (VIII, 727).

Obviously the pastoral setting is visually more beautiful than the industrial conglomerate but it seems unlikely that Galdós intended the contrast to indicate the superiority of the former when else-

[16]On the reverse of page 195 of the manuscript there is an earlier version of don Francisco's lament for the things his son cannot enjoy which gives greater emphasis to material elements. The latter include an 'alta posición', 'palacios', 'lujosos trenes', 'espectáculos públicos', 'los inmensos placeres de los viajes'.

where in the novel he constantly warns us not to judge by appearances. In reality, moreover, as Galdós was aware (see *8*, p. 32), the
industrial development in the North was not in conflict with ag-
riculture but promoted its development. He portrays not 'a savage
battle, between nature and science as Bly suggests (*37*, p. 54), but a
vision in which both nature and the achievements of man are worthy
of respect and admiration: like Teodoro, the reader is invited to
admire 'las distintas cosas que ya pasmaban por la grandeza de las
fuerzas naturales ya por el poder y brío del arte de los hombres' (IX,
729). Both Carlos and Teodoro challenge the mysteries of nature
and exploit its potential for the use of man: Carlos releases the
mineral wealth of the earth, Teodoro releases the vision which is
locked inside the blind Pablo. The fact that in both cases the consequences are not exclusively positive does not imply that Galdós
believed that man should leave nature well alone and that Pablo
would be better blind and the land unmined but rather, as Dendle
(*39*, p. 331) suggests, 'that unfortunate and unforseen consequences
accompany even the greatest advances of mankind'. 'Todos los grandes progresos traen su cortejo de pequeñas flaquezas', Galdós commented in 1870 (*9*, p. 128), and although these 'flaquezas' began to
assume greater importance in his work as he became progressively
more disillusioned with the materialistic ethos of bourgeois society,
he never rejected the idea of material progress. Indeed, he attributed
Spain's economic backwardness in relation to France to the 'extra-
viado juicio de un espiritualismo mal sano y rutinario que llevamos
desde inmemorial tiempo en el fondo de nuestro carácter' — an
attitude which equated poverty with 'honradez' and was incapable
of understanding 'que hay grandes Empresas, que negocian con inmensos capitales, y que el acertado empleo de éstos activando el
trabajo, trae la prosperidad y grandeza de las naciones'.[17] He did
not, however, share the widespread conviction that scientific and
material progress were inevitably accompanied by intellectual and
moral progress. In an article of 29 February 1872 he says: 'razón
habría para que templaran su entusiasmo los admiradores de la gene-
ración presente, que con una mano agujera los Alpes, canaliza el
istmo de Suez, sumerje[sic] los alambres eléctricos en el profundo

[17]'La moral y los negocios de Estado' (14 April 1887), in *Obras inéditas,*
ed. Alberto Ghiraldo, III (Madrid: Renacimiento, 1923), pp.299-310
(pp.299-300).

Océano, mientras que con la otra impele a los hombres a destrozarse unos a otros, en guerras estériles para la civilización y para el derecho' (*Crónica de la quincena*, p. 77). Such contradictions are presented in *Marianela* where the wonders of science and technology exist side by side with a girl whose deprivation of the cultural and intellectual benefits of civilization places her in the situation of primitive peoples. Like many nineteenth-century writers, Galdós wished to reconcile the spirit of enterprise, invention and individualism on which material progress rested with the more traditional values of caring and responsibility.

3 The Social Question

Introduction

The social question, as both nineteenth-century and modern critics
(*33*; *34*; *12*; *37*; *43*) have noted, is a central preoccupation in
Marianela. It dominates several chapters and is the focus of most of
the explicit moralizing in the novel: Galdós clearly regarded it as
sufficiently important to risk undermining the illusion of reality. He
does not, however, attempt to deal with all aspects of the social
question — a comprehensive concept which was used in the nineteenth century to refer not only to the struggle between capital and
labour but also to the general living and working conditions of the
lower classes. The areas he highlights and the solutions he explores
are determined chiefly by the historical context, his own middle-
class bias and the literary conventions within which he was writing.
This last aspect will be discussed more fully in Chapter 4; here I am
concerned principally with the ideological assumptions which con-
ditioned his approach.

In an interview in 1917 Galdós told Diego Montaner that he had
written the novel after a visit to the mines of Reocín, near Torrela-
vega: 'there, after I saw how the miners lived and appreciated what
their work in the galleries is, and what they themselves are like,
Socartes and Aldeacorba and Nela and Pablo were born' (*El Día
Gráfico*, 9 April 1917, quoted in *26*, II, p. 94: see also *8*, pp. 252-53
and 258). Though Galdós's initial inspiration was the brutal life of
the miners, as the statement indicates, he actually focused his novel
on two characters — Nela and Pablo — whose destinies are only
marginally related to the mines. There is, as several critics (*24*; *26*;
50) have observed, a curious disjunction between the setting and the
plot of the novel. Yet Galdós's remarks of 1917 were not those of an
older, politically more radical man misremembering the past in the
light of his current preoccupations. That he had been deeply im-
pressed by the degradation of the miners is evident in his allusions to
the subject in *Cuarenta leguas por Cantabria* (pp. 1445 and 1450), a
series of articles originally published in the *Revista de España* in

1876. Why did Galdós choose the mines as a backdrop for his novel but not explore in depth the living and working conditions of the miners? Why did he place the weight of the social theme on Marianela and not on Felipe? The answer, at least in part, lies in the historical context.

A serious preoccupation with the social question in Spain dates from the early 1870s when the development of the Spanish section of the International and the events of the Paris Commune of March-May 1871 led to intense public debate on the subject.[18] Interest continued throughout the decade and the subject for debate in the Sección de Ciencias Morales y Políticas of the Ateneo of Madrid in the session 1877-78 — when Galdós was writing *Marianela* — was 'Cuestiones que entrañan el problema social y medida en que toca su solución al individuo, a la sociedad y al Estado'.[19] Spain was, however, still predominantly an agricultural country, relatively free from industrial strife until the 1890s (*1*, p. 448). Moreover, despite the existence of child labour, the worst abuses of which the ineffectual law of 24 July 1873 attempted to control, the backwardness of Spanish industry made Felipe's case a far less common one than that of Nela. It was certainly one with which Galdós was personally less familiar; Nela, on the other hand, could have been taken from the streets of Madrid. When we consider that only a handful of novels about industrial life were published in the industrially far more advanced Victorian England, it should not surprise us that the Spanish novelist should deal somewhat summarily with the subject. [20]

There is, however, abundant contemporary testimony to the fact

[18]The First International - officially, the International Working Men's Association - was founded in London on 28 September 1864 by British and Continental labour leaders.

[19]Antonio Ruiz Salvador, *El Ateneo científico, literario y artístico de Madrid (1835-1885)* (London: Tamesis, 1971), pp.142-143. The debates, which were held on 15, 22 and 29 November, 6, 13 and 20 December 1877 and 3 January 1878, are reported in the *Boletín de Ateneo*, 2 (1878), 65-108. José Alvarez Junco, *La Comuna en España* (Madrid: Siglo XXI, 1971) dicusses the Spanish reaction to the Commune.

[20]The only major nineteenth-century Spanish novelist to attempt a detailed study of industrial life was Emilia Pardo Bazán who explored conditions in the tobacco factory in La Coruña in her novel *La tribuna* (1883). For the English novel see P.J. Keating, *The Working Classes in Victorian Fiction* (London: Routledge and Kegan Paul, 1979); Louis Cazamian, *The Social Novel in England, 1830-50*, translated with a foreword by Martin Fido (London: Routledge and Kegan Paul, 1973); Ivanka Kovacevic, *Fact into Fiction: English Literature and the Industrial Scene, 1750-1850* (Leicester University Press, 1975).

that the aspect of the social question which Galdós highlights – the plight of the uneducated, abandoned child – was a cause of great concern. Interest in the subject had been aroused by the publication in 1876 of the statistics for primary instruction for the period 1865-70. The dismal picture they presented provoked numerous articles in the press demanding the promotion of popular education and prompted some practical initiatives.[21] The Sociedad Económica Matritense, for example, gave its support in May 1877 to a society entitled Los Amigos de los Niños whose aim was to 'emprender una Santa Cruzada contra la miseria, la inmoralidad y la ignorancia que tantos estragos causa a la niñez'. The Matritense's report on the new society stressed the need to stem the loss of potential represented by the high child mortality rate and affirmed that Spain's ills would diminish only 'cuando hayamos puesto término a nuestra indiferencia y a nuestra incuria social, procurando arrancar de las manos de los desgraciados la fatal palanca del hambre y de la ignorancia'.[22]

The privileged place given to education in discussions on the social question was the product of a liberal tradition inherited from the Enlightenment which regarded universal education as a prerequisite for progress and social stability. Social revolution, crime, superstition, fanaticism were seen as the natural concomitants of ignorance: education was the panacea for all social ills. But liberal ideology, at least in its more radical version, regarded education as

[21] See for example M. Pedregal, 'La instrucción elemental en los pueblos modernos', *Revista Europea*, 9 (1877), 737-43 and 771-75; the subject was dealt with extensively by Sofía Tartilán in her *Páginas para la educación popular* (Madrid: Imprenta de Enrique Vicente, 1877) which was reviewed by Manuel de la Revilla in *RC*, 11 (1877), 373. Revilla returned to the subject a few months later, 'La emancipación del niño', *RC*, 16 (1878), 173-92. A royal decree of 1 March 1878 attempted to promote popular education by donating free books to rural schools, an initiative Teodoro Guerrero, 'Los ángeles desheredados', *La Época* (2 April 1878), urged 'las clases ilustradas' to support. In 1878 the Real Academia de Ciencias Morales y Políticas organized a competition on the theme: '¿La primera enseñanza deberá ser obligatoria, deberá ser gratuita? Medios más eficaces para obtener el cumplimiento de aquella obligación por las familias', *Memorias de la Real Academia de Ciencias Morales y Políticas*, 5 (1884), 23. The *memorias* of the three prizewinners – Concepción Arenal, Ricardo Molina and Rafael Monroy y Belmonte – were all subsequently published. There are of course literary antecedents for the theme of the uneducated, abandoned child, especially in the novels of Dickens: Philip Collins, *Dickens and Education* (London: Macmillan, 1963). Galdós himself returned to the subject in *La desheredada* (1881).

[22] 'Informe de la Comisión de la Sociedad Económica Matritense encargada de dar dictamen respecto a la Sociedad Los Amigos de los Niños, Mayo de 1877', *Revista de la Sociedad Económica Matritense*, 3 (1877), 392-94 (p. 393).

not merely a social need but an individual right which it was the
duty of family, society and the State to satisfy.[23] Not only was
access to education vital if each individual was to acquire a proper
sense of human dignity, it was essential for the proper working of a
society where, in theory at least, wealth, political influence and social prestige were the rewards for talent and hard work. In 1870
Galdós listed the benefits brought by the nineteenth century as follows:

> El ha traído la participación de todos en la vida pública, ha
> reconstituido el ser humano con la noción de la dignidad, del
> mérito personal, y,[...] ha traído la justicia de la gloria,
> [...] nos da a todos la seguridad de que si valemos hemos de ser
> apreciados,[...] nos abre el camino y nos paga con la estima-
> ción general, si la merecemos. (*9*, pp. 127-28)

Although Galdós was never to lose faith in this liberal ideal of a
meritocratic society, by the time he came to write *Marianela* he had
clearly modified his optimistic belief that the ideal had already been
realized. Indeed the novel can be read as an indictment of a society,
supposedly organized according to liberal principles, for its failure to
fulfil its promise to enable each individual to realize his or her potential.

Marianela

Marianela's childhood is set against a background of vices which
were regarded as characteristic of the lower classes: promiscuity,
alcoholism and suicide. An illegitimate child whose mother abandons
her to seek employment as a wet nurse in Madrid, she is initially
brought up by her father who is now cohabiting with her aunt. After
her father's death, her mother returns to work in the mines but is
dismissed for alcoholism and commits suicide. Totally uneducated
and physically retarded, Nela at sixteen has the appearance of a child
of twelve. She clearly suffers material deprivation. Teodoro describes

[23]For a general account of attitudes to education see Antonio Viñao Frago,
Política y educación en los orígenes de la España contemporánea (Madrid:
Siglo XXI, 1982), and Ivonne Turin, *La educación y la escuela en España de
1874 a 1902*, translated by Josefa Hernández Alonso (Madrid: Aguilar, 1967).

her as 'raquítica y mal alimentada' (III, 710) and, concerned for her physical welfare, he gives her money for shoes (XII, 740) and presses on her his own nourishing glass of milk (XI, 736). Florentina is horrified by the squalid conditions in which Nela lives, and is anxious to provide her with clothing and a proper bed (XVI, 751).

However, the novel focuses not on Nela's physical needs but on her emotional and intellectual wants. Nela herself is happy enough to sleep in her two baskets and go barefoot and, caring little for material things, she gladly gives the coins she receives to Felipe (IV, 714 and XII, 740). Galdós presents her as a child whose great potential has been wasted for lack of care, love and encouragement:

> Nunca se le dio a entender que tenía un alma pronta a dar ricos frutos si la cultivaba con esmero, ni que llevaba en sí, como los demás mortales, ese destello del eterno saber que se nombra inteligencia humana, y que de aquel destello podían salir infinitas luces y lumbre bienhechora. Nunca se le dio a entender que en su pequeñez fenomenal, llevaba en sí el germen de todos los sentimientos nobles y delicados, y que aquellos menudos brotes podían ser flores hermosísimas y lozanas, sin más cultivo que una simple mirada de vez en cuando. (IV, 716)

This view, which is expounded at length at the end of the novel by Teodoro (XXI, 769), is echoed by several other characters. Pablo comments on her 'disposición muy grande para conocer la verdad', a 'poderosa facultad[...] que sería primorosa si estuviera auxiliada por la razón y la educación' (VI, 722). Carlos has observed 'algo de inteligencia y agudeza de ingenio bajo aquella corteza de candor y salvaje rusticidad', and asserts that had someone taken the trouble to teach her, she probably would have been a better pupil than most boys (IX, 733). Don Francisco has noticed her 'modestia y delicadeza natural que es lástima que no haya sido cultivada' (XVII, 754). Her conduct throughout the novel amply justifies these comments. She is intelligent though uneducated, and as the narrator points out 'mostraba siempre buen sentido y sabía apreciar sesudamente las cosas de la vida' (XII, 742). Her generosity of spirit and moral rectitude are particularly evident in her attitude to those most responsible for her sufferings: the Centenos, Florentina and Pablo. Despite

the harsh treatment she receives from the Centenos, she counsels
Felipe not to blame his parents for their own ignorance and urges
him to send them letters and money when he is in Madrid (IV, 715
and XII, 741). Although she realizes she must lose Pablo to Florentina, she cannot bring herself to hate her rival and the faint traces of
antipathy and distrust give way to admiration and respect (XVI,
751). Much less can she blame Pablo for having deserted her, and she
finally joins together the hands of the couple whose union is her
own despair.

Nela's potential, however, has had no opportunity to flourish. Deprived of love, education and moral guidance, she is ignorant and
superstitious. Her religious ideas, analysed in detail in chapter XIII,
are described by Teodoro as 'vagas, monstruosas, equivocadas' (XXI,
769). With only nature as a guide, her moral ideas have resulted in a
pagan worship of beauty which exacerbates her own lack of self-
respect. Thus, left defenceless to cope with the tragedy that befalls
her, she sees suicide not as a sin but as the justifiable removal from
earth of an ugly and useless being (XIX, 760). There are, Teodoro
asserts, thousands more like Nela:

> ¿Quién los conoce? ¿Dónde están? Se pierden en los desiertos
> sociales . . . , que también hay desiertos sociales; en lo más
> obscuro de las poblaciones, en lo más solitario de los campos,
> en las minas, en los talleres. A menudo pasamos junto a ellos y
> no los vemos . . . Les damos limosna sin conocerlos . . . No po-
> demos fijar nuestra atención en esa miserable parte de la socie-
> dad. Al principio creí que la Nela era un caso excepcional;
> pero no, he meditado, he recordado, y he visto en ella un caso
> de los más comunes. Es un ejemplo del estado a que vienen los
> seres moralmente organizados para el bien, para el saber, para
> la virtud, y que por su abandono y apartamiento no pueden
> desarrollar las fuerzas del alma. (XXI, 769)

Marianela's individual situation thus provides a starting point for
a broader exploration of the social question and of the various attitudes and solutions offered by contemporary society. Galdós clearly regards society in general as responsible for Nela's plight. Using
Teodoro as his spokesman, he passionately denounces it for failing

to provide her with even the minimum of schooling and religious instruction which were supposedly available to all (XIX, 762). Like his admired Dickens, Galdós, in *Marianela* at least, shows himself to be a committed interventionist on social matters. In an authorial comment he asserts that Nela is entitled to 'ciertas atenciones' not due to those with health, family and home, but which correspond 'por jurisprudencia cristiana al inválido, al pobre, al huérfano y al desheredado' (IV, 716). These words clearly indicate that Galdós believed that the solution to the social question should be based on the Christian ethic with its emphasis on brotherly love and care for the weak. In his survey of attitudes to the social question he reserves his sharpest criticism for false charity, a theme which has been studied by several critics (*37; 43; 49*).

Galdós's two chief targets are self-important charity and a charity which attends only to material needs. La Señana is guilty of both. She regards her generosity to Nela as bordering on heroism and frequently congratulates herself on having earned her 'puestecito en el cielo'. She fails to realize, says the narrator, that 'una palabra cariñosa, un halago, un trato delicado y amante, que hicieran olvidar al pequeño su pequeñez, al miserable su miseria, son heroismos de más precio que el bodrio sobrante de una mala comida' (IV, 716). These points are developed further in chapter IX in the discussion between Sofía and Teodoro which arises out of an incident designed to place Sofía in a bad light. Heedless of Nela's safety, Sofía sends the girl scrambling down the cave of la Trascava to rescue her precious toy terrier, Lilí, purchased in London at the cost of 200 *duros*. The dog itself is used to satirize Sofía's absurdly exaggerated concern – '¡Ay, señora, pero qué boba es usted!', it seems to say to her (IX, 732). Teodoro suggests that Sofía's time and money would be better spent on buying shoes for Nela rather than a coat for Lilí. The ensuing discussion shows that Sofía views the poor as almost less than human, indeed she even questions God's wisdom in allowing people like Nela and her mother to survive. She regards the poor as personally responsible for their vices and, therefore, undeserving of compassion. For her, the problem is one of statistics not human beings. The solutions she supports involve little personal sacrifice or commitment on her part. Thus, although she spends a good deal of her time organizing raffles, masked balls, bullfights, cockfights and dramatic functions for the benefit of the poor, such activities are social rather than charitable, providing amusement for the rich rather than funds for the poor. Even don Manuel, a great admirer of Sofía's charitable activities, admits that most of the profits are swallowed up by the expenses of organizing such functions (XXI, 768). Other solutions she supports are 'asilos de beneficencia' for the destitute and religion for those who have reached the limits of despair.

Sofía's activities and attitudes to the social question are the conventional ones of her society. They are based on a rigid sense of class distinction which denies any common humanity between rich and poor, an aspect which is highlighted in Galdós's treatment of don Manuel. Don Manuel is exasperated by his daughter's unconventional mode of practising charity. Her excessive familiarity with Marianela — making her clothes, bringing her to the house — he regards as a lack of good breeding ('buena educación'), which, according to him, consists largely of the need to treat each person according to his or her social position, 'no dando a ninguna ni más ni menos de lo que correspondía con arreglo al fuero social' (XIV, 747).

Teodoro regards the solutions supported by Sofía and don Manuel as inadequate because they are aimed at fulfilling material rather than spiritual and intellectual needs and because they fail to search for the causes of suffering. For Teodoro, it is society itself which breeds the vices it is so quick to condemn. Unlike Sofía who transfers responsibility for the solution to anonymous agencies — charitable associations, welfare institutions, religion — Teodoro stresses the importance of personal contact. Charitable associations, he says, are ineffectual if their members never even ask the poor what causes their suffering; the asylums can never provide that family affection which inspires a sense of dignity and self-respect; religion is useless to the ignorant who have no 'amigo inteligente', or 'maestro' or priest to advise them (IX, 733). So great is the importance he attaches to the role of the individual, that he suggests as a solution to the problem of 'la miseria infantil' that every orphan should have the right to be adopted by a childless, well-to-do couple (IX, 734), a solution which possibly seems less bizarre today than it did in 1878.

Don Francisco Penáguilas and his son Pablo play a less prominent role in the social theme. Although they escape the satire Galdós directs at Sofía and don Manuel, they too, or at least don Francisco, could be said to illustrate the social indifference which Teodoro attacks so sharply (*37; 43*). Nela has been Pablo's guide for over 18 months yet don Francisco has done little to either educate her or improve her material conditions. It is only at this point that Pablo determines to ask his father to do these things (VI, 722). Don Francisco's sense of class distinction is less overt than that of his brother and he is more kindly disposed to Nela than Sofía, but he is often insensitive to her feelings. For example, he ridicules in her presence Pablo's conviction that she is beautiful (XI, 737). He does not regard himself as having any obligations beyond giving her scraps from his kitchen or a few coins; all his care and attention is lavished on his son. Pablo is well aware of Nela's good qualities and provides her with the love and affection which allow her to blossom in his company (VI, 720). Yet he too finally deserts her and in a sense, this abandonment, more cruel than any other, symbolizes the indifference of which she has been a victim all her life.

Leopoldo Alas saw in Florentina 'una niña hermosa como ninguna, por dentro y por fuera, del alma y del cuerpo' (*31*, p. 68), a view echoed by some modern critics (*12*; *26*; *49*) who regard her as the vehicle of Galdós's message. It is true that from the beginning Florentina treats Nela with affection and seems to embody that sense of personal concern and responsibility Teodoro found lacking in Sofía. She recognizes the need to give the poor 'aquella limosna que vale más que todos los mendrugos y todos los trapos imaginables, y es la consideración, la dignidad, el nombre' (XVI, 751). Appalled by inequalities — '¿Por qué esta pobre huérfana ha de ser descalza y yo no?' (XV, 748) — she claims that her sympathies are with 'los que quieren que se reparta por igual todo lo que hay en el mundo' (XV, 748). However, as some critics (*37; 43; 47; 53*) have pointed-ed out, there is evidence in the text to suggest that Galdós was not entirely uncritical of her. There is undoubtedly a constant contradiction between what Florentina says and what she does. Despite her stated desire to break down class barriers and make Nela her sister, she consistently behaves with a patronizing condescension which reaffirms class differences. She addresses Nela as 'huerfanita', suggests she will probably be ungrateful for what she does for her (XV, 749), laments in Nela's presence that no one has ever cared for her

(XV, 749), and tells her that she is the 'pobre más pobre' she has promised to care for if Pablo's sight is restored (XVI, 751). For Florentina, Nela is an object of charity, her very own 'pobre' to be transformed into a *señorita* like herself and, although she has more warmth of heart than Sofía, she never attempts to discover what Nela herself feels or wants. Thus, when Pablo recovers his sight, Florentina unwittingly increases Nela's sufferings by her constant allusions to his worship of physical beauty and her hints of their forthcoming marriage. Her amazed reaction to Nela's assurance that the latter does not hate her and her inability to understand why the girl runs away instead of coming to collect her reward, show that she acts out of ignorance and insensitivity rather than calculated malice (XVII, 754). There is, moreover, a good deal of self-interest behind Florentina's charity. She frequently draws attention to her own generosity, though it is perhaps too harsh to dismiss her charity as a mere pose (*47*, p. 43). Her amateur dressmaking efforts on Nela's behalf, for example, betray her preoccupation with her own image (XXI, 767), since, as she admits, Nela would be better dressed by a professional seamstress, as of course Florentina herself is. The self-serving element is evident too in her reactions to Nela's flight — the disappearance of 'la más risueña ilusión de su vida' (XVII, 755) — and to her death — 'yo quería hacerla feliz y ella no quería serlo' (XXI, 774). Her self-esteem is finally satisfied when she pays for a lavish funeral for Nela and erects a magnificent tomb to her memory.

We should, however, beware of over-emphasizing the negative aspects of Florentina's approach. A modern reader probably finds her patronizing airs more offensive than her creator did; nor can we completely discount the possibility that her insensitive declaration of her charitable intentions in Nela's presence may obey the demands of didacticism rather than those of characterization. There can be little doubt that Florentina stands as a favourable contrast to Sofía and don Manuel. Whereas they are clearly censured through satire, it is more difficult to identify with precision Galdós's attitude to Florentina. Her goodness is exalted by many characters and even the apparently futile gesture of the tomb is presented from two different points of view: 'algún positivista empedernido criticóla por esto; pero no faltó quien viera en tan desusado hecho una prueba más de la delicadeza de su alma' (XXII, 774). The only explicit criticism is the narrator's mildly reproving observation that her immense goodness frequently incapacitated her judgement (XVII, 754). Though Florentina's inexperience and ignorance of the true situation prevent her from properly implementing her ideal, there can, I think, be little doubt that Galdós placed high value on the ideal itself. If, as Bly says (*37*), Florentina's charitable works might have been beneficial in another case, but fail miserably with Nela, it is because they come too late. Nela herself is distraught at her inability to accept Florentina's offer:

> ¡Ver realizado lo que tantas veces viera en sus sueños palpitando de gozo y tener que renunciar a ello! . . . ¡Sentirse llamada por una voz cariñosa, que le ofrecía fraternal amor, hermosa vivienda, consideración, nombre, bienestar y no poder acudir e este llamamiento, inundada de gozo, de esperanza, de gratitud! . . . ¡Rechazar la mano celestial que la sacaba de aquella sentina de degradación y miseria para hacer de la vagabunda una persona y elevarla de la jerarquía de los animales domésticos a la de los seres respetados y queridos! (XVII, 752-53)

The mature judgement Florentina lacks is to be found in Teodoro who discovers the cause of Nela's suffering and proposes to save her by giving her the education and moral guidance she has so far lacked. He wants to give her a sense of dignity, correct her excessive worship of beauty and convince her that 'hay una porción de dones más estimables que el de la hermosura, dones del alma que ni son ajados por el tiempo, ni están sujetos al capricho de los ojos' (XIX, 761). By encouraging the virtues of humility and abnegation he hopes to give her the strength to cope with her disappointment. He tells her: 'aprenderás a poner tu fealdad a los pies de la hermosura, a contemplar con serenidad y alegría los triunfos ajenos, a cargar de cadenas ese gran corazón tuyo para que jamás vuelva a sentir envidia ni despecho, para que ame a todos por igual, poniendo por cima de todos a los que te han hecho daño. Entonces serás lo que debes ser por tu natural condición y por las cualidades que desde el nacer posees' (XIX, 762).

Modern readers have, understandably enough, found this scene irritating, if not painful: Krebs (*43*) dismisses Teodoro's disquisition as absurd and 'insoportable' and Bly (*37*) argues that Teodoro, failing to appreciate Nela's real needs, proposes a disastrously inappropriate solution. However, in a note in the manuscript (p. 341) Galdós refers to the exchange as a 'gran diálogo filosófico moral, el nervio de la novela', and a close examination of the scene confirms that its purpose is not to characterize Teodoro as a heartless pedant but to underscore the moral lesson. The fact that the text draws attention to the inopportuneness of Teodoro's moralizing while at the same time expressing approval of his sentiments suggests that Galdós was uncomfortably aware that his didactic intention was detrimental to the plausibility of the scene. Nela responds to Teodoro's 'sensatas palabras' with eyes which seem to say 'Pero ¿a qué vienen todas estas sabidurías, señor pedante?' (XIX, 761). It cannot be affirmed, the narrator states, that Nela understood Teodoro's speech, since he had momentarily forgotten to whom he was talking, 'pero la vagabunda sentía una fascinación singular, y las ideas de aquel hombre penetraban dulcemente en su alma' – the results of 'el potente y fatal dominio que la inteligencia superior ejerce sobre la inferior' (XIX, 762). Nela's attempted suicide and the physical and psychological collapse which ensue confirm Teodoro's contention that a lack of education and love have terrible consequences. If Teodoro's solution is inappropriate for Nela, it is because, like that of Florentina, it comes too late. Her character and beliefs are already formed and her emotions are irrevocably engaged with a man she can never marry. Even Pablo's influence, the narrator asserts, came too late to change the fundamental basis of her philosophy (XIII, 742). That basis is the high value she attaches to physical beauty which, in her mind, justifies both Pablo's desertion and her own suicide. The very fact that the solutions are too late is an integral part of the moral lesson of the novel: that society's failure to fulfil its responsibilities results in a tragic waste of human potential.

For Nela, the only solution is death, as Teodoro himself comes to realize: his final words before her corpse are 'Mujer has hecho bien en dejar este mundo' (XXI, 774). It has been suggested that the simple remedy for Nela's plight would have been Pablo's love (*37*; *49*), but this is in fact impossible – and not only because his worship of physical beauty has made him fall in love with Florentina. The romantic framework of the novel — the heroine with the ugly body and the beautiful soul whose idyllic romance with the blind Pablo is doomed when he recovers his sight — diverts attention from the fact that the relationship is doomed anyway. Even had Nela not been ugly, it is highly improbable that there would ever have been a marriage between the penniless, illiterate, illegitimate daughter of an alcoholic mine-worker and the only son, whether blind or sighted, of a wealthy landowner. No one, except Nela and Pablo, both of whom are presented as having distorted views of reality, ever considers the possibility of such a match. Indeed, its improbability within the conventions of bourgeois society goes a long way to explaining why Florentina at times seems so insensitive to Nela's feelings and why it takes Teodoro so long to get to the root of her distress. The natural match is between Florentina and Pablo, two cousins of the same social class and background, whose marriage will consolidate the newly inherited wealth of their fathers. Despite the fact that don Manuel in his letter to his brother emphasizes the economic basis of the proposed union — 'casaré a mi Florentina con tu Pablo, y aquí tienes colocado a interés compuesto el medio millón del primo Faustino' (XI, 738) — there is no suggestion that this would be a sordid marriage of convenience. On the contrary, don Francisco describes to his friends a future full of touching scenes of bourgeois domesticity: 'he visto una especie de Paraíso en la Tierra . . . , he visto un joven y alegre matrimonio; he visto ángeles, nietecillos alrededor de mí.' He ends his account of his hopes by wiping away a tear with 'la mano basta y ruda, endurecida por el arado' and his friends remain silent, 'hondamente impresionados por la relación patética y sencilla del bondadoso padre' (XI, 738-39). Robert Kirsner argues that in *Marianela* 'se enfoca el matrimonio con brutalidad y aspereza' (*22*, p. 59) but the Dickensian sentimentality of this scene, together with the fact that there is never any doubt that Pablo and Florentina do love each other precludes, I think, any suggestion that Galdós intends to contrast bourgeois marriage unfavourably with romantic love.

Casares (*59*) points to the implausibility of Pablo having been so totally unaware of the impossibility of a match with Nela and suggests that Galdós's desire to make all his characters 'simpáticos y nobles' led him to 'escamotear[...] muchas verdades'. There is undoubtedly some substance to this charge of evasion: both the weight of the philosophical symbolism and the romantic focus of the novel tend to obscure the fact that ultimately Nela is a victim of the class system. A genuine solution to her problem would require measures more drastic than those proposed by Florentina and Teodoro and less easily accommodated within the existing structure of society.

The Centeno Family

Despite the sense of irreparable waste created by Nela's death, the basic framework of the novel is not pessimistic but optimistic. It may be too late for Nela but for others there is still time: 'para ti es tiempo, para mí es tarde' (XVIII, 756), she sadly tells Felipe as she refuses to accompany him on his journey to Madrid in search of an education and a future. It is significant that the novel ends on a note of hope not despair, not with Nela's death but with Felipe's escape: 'al fin le vemos, allí está, pequeño, mezquino, atomístico. Pero tiene alientos y logrará ser grande' (XXII, 775). Felipe thus represents a hope for the future and as such he serves as an important foil to Marianela (*45*, p. 250).

As we have seen, Galdós's choice of Nela rather than Felipe as the chief focus of the social problem allows him to highlight the moral aspects of his theme: charity and education. But even in his treatment of Felipe these aspects are uppermost. Felipe is only twelve; he has never attended school and he spends twelve hours a day 'en el embrutecedor trabajo de las minas' (IV, 715). Keenly aware of the dehumanizing nature of his life, he tells Nela:

> No somos gente, sino animales. A veces se me pone en la cabe-
> za que somos menos que las mulas, y yo me pregunto si me
> diferencio en algo de un borrico . . . Coger una cesta llena de
> mineral y echarla en un vagón; empujar el vagón hasta los hor-
> nos; revolver con un palo el mineral que se está lavando.
> ¡Ay! . . . – al decir esto, los sollozos cortaban la voz del infeliz
> muchacho –. ¡Cór . . . , córcholis!, el que pase muchos años
> en este trabajo, al fin se ha de volver malo, y sus sesos serán de
> calamina. (IV, 714)

Galdós's principal target, however, is not the inhuman working conditions of the mines. These are alluded to only briefly in this account and in the following chapter, 'Trabajo, Paisaje, Figura', where, moreover, the focus is on the machinery rather than the men. Felipe is presented, not as a victim of a capitalist system which permits and even encourages child labour, but as the victim of his own parents' avarice.

Despite the parents' assertion that they are too poor to allow him to leave the mines and attend school, it is clear that they exploit his labour and that of their other children out of greed not need. Their present income, the narrator asserts, would have seemed to them a 'fortuna de príncipes' in their days as tinkers (IV, 715). La Señana, the very incarnation of cupidity, weighs their money 'con embriagador deleite' (XII, 740) and views the arrival of the weekly wages as though they were 'el propio Jesús sacramentado' (IV, 715) entering her house. She offers her children few material comforts in exchange for the 'hacienda' they are making for her and is even more resolutely hostile to spending money on 'pasto intelectual'. Her love for her children is conditional upon their unquestioningly accepting work in the mines, bringing home their wages and not entertaining 'aspiraciones locas ni afán de lucir galas, ni de casarse antes de tiempo, ni de aprender diabluras, ni de meterse en sabidurías, "porque los pobres —decía— siempre han de ser pobres, y como pobres portarse, sin farolear como los ricos y gente de la ciudad, que estaba todo comida de vicios y podrida de pecados" ' (IV, 716). This rationalization of her own greed thus makes her a spokeswoman of social immobility.

Thus the life of 'atroz y degradante miseria' in which the family lives and the ignorance to which the children are condemned is entirely the fault of the parents. This view of the lower classes was not uncommon: Pi y Margall, President of the First Republic, introduced the 1873 law restricting the working hours for children as a measure designed principally to protect the latter against the 'abusos' of their parents. The charge was dismissed as 'calumniosa y criminal' by the anarchist newspaper, *El Condenado* (21 June 1873), which argued that the evils of child labour were the result of the 'inicua organización social' which forced parents to send their children out to work in order that the family might earn enough to survive. It is strange, as Pattison (*50*, p. 128) points out, that Galdós, despite his conviction that society was largely responsible for the degradation of the

poor, should have made the Centeno family so despicable and not
sought to explain their baseness and avarice by shifting the blame
onto society. The only hint that they are not responsible for their
attitudes comes from Marianela who urges Felipe to forgive them,
since if they are unwilling to educate him 'es porque no tienen talento' (XII, 741). Galdós's presentation of the Centenos' ignorance is,
however, consistently satirical and without any trace of compassion.
The father's head, he affirms, 'en opinión de muchos, rivalizaba en
dureza con el martillo pilón montado en los talleres' (IV, 715).
Nevertheless, La Señana firmly believes that with her husband's
erudition, 'adquirida en copiosas lecturas, tenía bastante la familia
para merecer el dictado de sapientísima' (IV, 715). The father's
attempts to read are described with patronizing irony: his trembling
and quivering finger follows the lines of print 'para poder guiar su
espíritu por aquel laberinto de letras'; phrases disintegrate into
words, words into syllables until he extinguishes the light 'a cuyo
resplandor había enriquecido sus conocimientos' (IV, 713; see also
XII, 740).

Not only is there no sympathy for the Centeno parents, but they
are presented as representative examples of what the author regards
as the most destructive and terrible enemy of society: 'la codicia del
aldeano'. In a long authorial intervention he roundly condemns this
'positivismo de las aldeas' which kills all noble ambition and locks
millions 'en el círculo de una existencia mecánica, brutal y tene-
brosa' (IV, 714). For the avaricious peasant, he continues, there is
neither moral law nor religion, all is superstition and 'cálculos grose-
ros', he is 'la bestia más ignoble que puede imaginarse'. 'La ignorancia, la rusticidad, la miseria en el vivir' complete the portrait of a
man capable of reducing the whole moral order, conscience and the
soul to numbers (IV, 715). Responsibility for sordid and brutal
living conditions is thus deflected from social organization onto
individual moral failings.

Although such greed undoubtedly existed, the fact that Galdós
selects it to the exclusion of all other potential causes, social or
economic, suggests an unwillingness to explore possibilities which
might challenge existing social structures. The moral focus and the
contradiction noted by Pattison are the consequences of Galdós's

bourgeois perspective. As a political liberal Galdós supports social reform not social revolution; his ideal is not a classless society but a society ordered according to talent and merit. His concern is less with the lower classes as a whole than with those members of them whose intelligence, sensitivity or noble ambition entitle them to rise above the common mass of men, that is, the Marianelas, the Felipes and the Golfines. His scant sympathy for those bereft of such qualities can be seen in his treatment of the Centeno offspring. All, except Felipe, have apathetically accepted their degraded condition and show no desire 'de otra vida mejor y más digna de seres inteligentes' (IV, 715). Mariuca and Pepina, described by Teodoro as 'bestias en forma humana' (XIX, 759), are distinguished only by their youth and robust physique. Tanasio, 'un hombre apático', whose lack of character and ambition border on 'idiotismo', was born 'dispuesto a ser máquina' and has become 'la herramienta más grosera'. If he were ever to have an idea of his own, the narrator concludes, 'se cambiaría el orden admirable de todas las cosas, por el cual ninguna piedra puede pensar' (IV, 715). The description of the Centenos as the 'familia de piedra' patently indicates their total lack of any spiritual, moral or intellectual aspirations.[24] The author and his spokesman Teodoro have nothing but disdain for the mechanical labour in which they are engaged. '¿Acaso hemos nacido para trabajar como animales?' (XIX, 759), Teodoro rhetorically asks Marianela in an attempt to persuade her that her intelligence and sensitivity have destined her for better things than breaking stone and carting earth like Mariuca and Pepina. Earlier he criticizes Sofía for her failure to give the poor a sense of dignity 'haciéndoles pasar del bestial trabajo mecánico al trabajo de la inteligencia' (IX, 733). But not all can make that transition, or else who would work the mines? The contradiction in Galdós's analysis – the ignorance of Nela is society's responsibility, that of the Centenos is their own responsibility – means that the question of whether the system itself actually requires vast numbers of menial labourers is never posed. Implicit in the denunciation of the Centenos is the view that they deserve the kind of life they lead.

[24]In the manuscript version Galdós crossed out references to another even more brutish Centeno son called Zoiló who he described as 'cruel, borracho, sensual, pendenciero . . . los vicios espoleando un alma soñolienta de origen y embrutecida en las minas' (p. 72).

Only Felipe, usually referred to by the diminutive 'Celipín', merits the author's sympathy. Morally and intellectually superior to his siblings, he has the drive and ambition they lack. Despite the fact that, unlike them, he has not even had the benefit of a rudimentary primary education, he clearly perceives the brutality of their lives and aspires to an education and a career. He is, moreover, the only member of the family to appreciate Nela's moral and intellectual worth. For him, she is 'más buena que María santísima' (XII, 740). He is of course grateful for the money she gives him, but there is no doubt as to the sincerity of his affection. He urges her to join him in his escape to Madrid because she too has 'talento' and could become a 'señora' as he intends to become a 'caballero' (XII, 741). When he leaves Socartes he risks discovery of his own flight in a final attempt to persuade her to accompany him. When she refuses he offers her a peseta and swallowing down his tears sets off (XVIII, 757). His moral calibre is evident too in his attitude to his parents. Although at first he claims not to love them because of the brutal life they have imposed on the family (IV, 714), he heeds Nela's advice and promises to write and send them presents from Madrid. His pleasure at embarking on a new life is mingled with sadness when he thinks how they will weep at his departure (XVIII, 756).

Felipe's models are Carlos and especially Teodoro Golfín. So great is his admiration for the latter that he determines to imitate him in every detail, from living in a 'casa de trapo viejo' to working as a barber and finally becoming a doctor. This ambition is presented in a delightfully absurd dream which combines visions of amazing medical prowess — se veía a sí mismo[...] arrancando criaturas a la muerte mediante copiosas tomas de mosquitos cogidos por una doncella y guisados un lunes con palos de mimbres' — with visions of an equally amazing social success in which, dressed in rich clothes, he is solicited by royalty, praised by magnates and carried in triumph through the cities of the world (XII, 742). It is wrong, I think, to interpret Felipe's exaggerated visions of material splendour and his vanity with regard to his own abilities as a negative judgement by Galdós on his character and aspirations (*37; 28*, p. 145, note 1). The dream and Felipe's childish boasts emphasize his ignorance and naiveté and are used principally for comic effect. Moreover, it is important to note that, unlike his parents who begrudge every penny spent on material comforts, Felipe intends to use his earnings to make life pleasant for himself and his family. He plans to send them lavish gifts (XII, 741) and quite rightly senses that the frock coat, hat, shoes and gloves he intends to purchase for himself are indispensable signs of social respectability. Nor do his aspirations remain at the level of idle dreams. Denied a schooling by his parents, he decides to take the initiative and buy a 'cartilla' to teach himself to read (IV, 714), and finally he has the courage and determination to escape his sordid background. As he disappears into the night, the author gives his seal of approval: 'la Geología había perdido una piedra, y la sociedad había ganado un hombre' (XVIII, 757).

The Golfín Brothers

In chapter X, 'Historia de dos hijos del pueblo', a title which stresses the humble origins of the Golfín brothers, Teodoro recounts the story of their life so that it may serve as an example for 'todos los desamparados, todos los niños perdidos' (X, 735). It is a tale of will-power, perseverance, initiative and hard work. Born into the lowest class, they struggled from their earliest years to escape poverty and ignorance, and with determination steadily climbed up the social hierarchy. At the time of the action of the novel they are both materially well off and professionally well established, Carlos as a mining engineer and Teodoro as a famous eye surgeon. Teodoro sees himself as a modern *conquistador* and concludes his review of their past with the words 'yo había sido una especie de Colón, el Colón del trabajo, una especie de Hernán Cortés; yo había descubierto en mí un Nuevo Mundo, y, después de descubrirlo, lo había conquistado' (X, 736). His brother enthusiastically assents: 'si hay héroes en el mundo, tú eres uno de ellos.'

Teodoro is certainly a modern bourgeois hero and his story would merit a place in the vast body of success literature which was so popular in the middle decades of the nineteenth century. The most important example of the genre was Samuel Smiles's *Self-Help* (1859), which had sold a quarter of a million copies by the end of the century. Such literature was designed to provide readers with sound values and good advice about how to get on in life and usually

cited examples of the achievements of self-made men as illustrations
of what each man might do for himself.[25] The doctrine of self-help
had no lack of supporters in Spain. The Sociedad Económica
Matritense, for example, inaugurated its 'Conferencias dominicales'
for workers in 1879 with a lecture on the subject. The speaker,
Valentín Morán, produced an impressive list of self-made men,
including some Spaniards, so that they might serve as an inspiration
for his audience.[26] Morán stressed the importance of education, as
did Rafael María de Labra in another lecture on the theme of self-
help delivered in the Ateneo Mercantil de Madrid in October 1878.
Those who were most concerned with the moral and material
improvement of the masses, Labra asserted, asked them '¿queréis
ser, queréis vivir, queréis influir, queréis mandar? ¡Pues *Ilustraos!*'.
The 'fórmula de nuestros tiempos' was, he continued, 'ser inteligentes para ser ricos y libres'.[27]

Galdós, like Labra, attached great importance to education as an
instrument of self-advancement. For Teodoro, instruction takes pre-
cedence over material comforts: when Carlos asks him for bread, he
gives him mathematics (X, 735), and when the doctor tells him to
send his brother to the country to recuperate, he sends him to the
Escuela de Minas. Nor is instruction merely a means to an end:
neither Carlos nor Teodoro is content with mere material success.
On the contrary, both are devoted to their professions: Carlos is
'apasionado por la Mineralogía y la Metalurgia' (IX, 730) and
Teodoro's enthusiasm for his profession is everywhere evident.

[25] See Asa Briggs's introduction to the Centenary edition of Smiles's *Self-Help*
(London: John Murray, 1958). A Spanish version of *Self-Help* was published
in 1876: *Los hombres de energía y coraje: notas biográficas tomadas del
popular libro titulado 'Self-Help'* (Madrid: Imprenta de Aurelio J. Alaria,
1876).

[26] 'Conferencias dominicales', *Revista de la Sociedad Económica Matritense*, 5
(1879), 28-31. Morán was secretary of the Sociedad.

[27] Labra, 'El esfuerzo individual: discurso pronunciado en la inauguración del
curso académico de 1878-79 del Ateneo Mercantil de Madrid, Octubre de
1878', in *Discursos políticos, académicos y forenses*, 1st series (Madrid:
Imprenta de Aurelio J. Alaria, 1884), p. 206. Labra was a tireless propagand-
ist in favour of popular education. Galdós was a member of the same *tertulia*
in the Ateneo de Madrid as Labra and other Krausist figures: see Luis Antón
del Olmet and Arturo García Carrafa, *Galdós* (Madrid: Imprenta de 'Alrededor
del Mundo', 1912), p. 65.

There seems to be little evidence to support the view that they are 'followers of nineteenth-century materialism', whose history suggests that material prosperity has led them to 'moral ruin' (*37*, p. 61). On the contrary, Teodoro's experiences have given him a highly developed social conscience and a sensitivity to the needs of others. He discovers more about Marianela and makes more effort to give her practical help in the few days he is in Aldeacorba than the rural patriarch, don Francisco Penáguilas, has done in the eighteen months she has been his son's guide. It is true that Teodoro is proud of his own and his brother's achievements, and he confesses his own lack of modesty with a refreshing frankness (X, 735). However, the narrator explicitly condones his vanity as 'la más disculpable de todas las vanidades, pues consistía en sacar a relucir sus dos títulos de gloria, a saber: su pasión por la Cirurgía y la humildad de su origen' (IX, 730). His proud boasting of the brothers' humble lineage is in fact favourably contrasted with Sofía's snobbish desire to conceal their modest origins. Teodoro's pride is not egoistic as has been suggested (*37*), for he would like others to follow his example. Nor has success made him, as it made many other self-made men, smugly self-satisfied, content to attribute the failure of others to a weakness of character. Although he subscribes to the maxim with which Smiles opened his *Self-Help* — 'Heaven helps those who help themselves' — he recognizes that there are many who can do little without help from others. Like so many of the doctors in Galdós's work, Teodoro acts as the novelist's mouthpiece on matters of social reform.

If anything, Teodoro is something of an idealized figure and his success story certainly has a touch of the fairy tale about it. The educational system of mid-nineteenth-century Spain, far from encouraging social mobility, used the cost of education to perpetuate a stratified social structure. Instruction was free only at the primary level for the very poor and tuition fees rose in proportion to the level of instruction. It is very unlikely that Teodoro's small wages would have sufficed to pay for his own medical studies and for his brother's tuition at the prestigious and elitist Escuela de Minas. Entry into the latter was very difficult and fewer than a dozen students graduated every year. The possibility of a boy who had worked as a grocer's messenger boy and as a barber's assistant gaining a place in competition with the sons of the privileged and well-connected must have been exceedingly remote.[28] *El doctor Centeno* (1883) gives a much more realistic account of the difficulties facing a poor boy who wished to acquire an education.[29] This is far from the novel of the self-made man which Galdós seems to promise at the end of *Marianela* and it exposes quite clearly the inadequacy of the self-help ethic. But even in the more optimistic *Marianela*, it is obvious that Galdós did not regard self-help as a panacea for the social question. Teodoro's success is not due solely to his own dogged perseverance and initiative. As he himself admits, 'Dios me protegía, dándome siempre buenos amos'; thus his way is eased by the encouragement and material aid of kindly employers. A small legacy providentially appears when he is at the beginning of his career, enabling him to pay for his brother's books and to acquire the decent clothes he himself needs to attract patients (X, 736).It is, moreover, clear that, although Teodoro's example may serve as an inspiration and model for some, it is of little use to others. Marianela lacks the initiative and self-confidence which enable Felipe to make his escape. The conviction of her own uselessness, together with the emotional ties which bind her to Socartes, prevent her from leaving. Of course, even if she had the will-power to make the break, her sex would preclude her from the glittering prospect of a successful career, as even the twelve-year-old Felipe can see when he promises to teach her a little of what he learns: 'un poquito nada más, porque las mujeres no necesitan tantas sabidurías como nosotros los señores médicos' (XVIII, 756).

Galdós and Krausist Social Philosophy

Galdós's treatment of the social question has been criticized for being superficial and sentimental (*12*, p. 216; *47*, p. 66; *48*, pp. 144-45) but we cannot, as Hinterhäuser points out (*21*, p. 205), demand

[28]For the Escuela de Minas see Mariano Peset and José Luis Peset, *La universidad española (siglos XVIII y XIX): despotismo ilustrado y revolución liberal* (Madrid: Taurus, 1974), pp.451-54 and 643-44. León Roch, the protagonist of Galdós's *La familia de León Roch,* is also educated at the Escuela de Minas but he comes from a prosperous background, as does Pepe Rey (*Doña Perfecta*), another engineer.

[29]Geraldine M. Scanlon, '*El doctor Centeno*: A Study in Obsolescent Values', *Bulletin of Hispanic Studies*, 55 (1978), 245-53.

of the novelist a modern point of view. A bourgeois liberal, Galdós provides an analysis which excludes the possibility of a revolutionary reorganization of the existing structure of society, but this does not make him a reactionary or a conservative. The solutions to the social question proposed by nineteenth-century bourgeois society embraced a political spectrum which went from a traditional conservative Catholic remedy of charity from the rich and resignation from the poor, through the laissez-faire policy of non-intervention espoused by economic liberalism, to the social reformism of radical liberalism. In *Marianela*, Galdós exposes the first solution, whose spokeswoman is Sofía, as inadequate; explicitly and implicitly condemns the second; and adopts a position close to the third. The sentimental humanitarianism of the novel is reminiscent of the propaganda of democrats and republicans whose stock reading-matter in the 1860s and 70s was Eugène Sue and his Spanish imitators, the early Hugo, Lamartine and Lammenais (*3*, p. 83). While the tone of emotional protest in the novel derives from social romanticism, the ideas themselves are very similar to those of the most advanced bourgeois thinkers of the period: the Krausist intellectuals, several of whom were active in republican politics.

The most comprehensive and coherent expression of Krausist social reformism is to be found in the works of Gumersindo de Azcárate. The Krausists saw social reform primarily in ethical terms: Christian ideals and tenets were to serve as moral imperatives. Thus, Azcárate asserts, the first condition of social reform is 'la restauración del decálogo en las conciencias, y en la vida el cumplimiento de los deberes en todos, principalmente en las clases directoras'.[30]

Azcárate was, however, careful to distance himself from a tradi-

[30]'Estudio sobre el problema social', in his *Estudios económicos y sociales*, 2nd ed. (Madrid: Victoriano Suárez, 1876), pp.113-58 (p.142), abbreviated in subsequent references in the text to *EES*. Other abbreviations used in the text correspond to the following works by Azcárate: *Minuta: Minuta de un testamento* (Madrid: Victoriano Suárez, 1876); *Resumen; Resumen de un debate sobre el problema social* (Madrid: Gras y Compañía, 1881). The latter was a series of articles published in the *Revista de España* in 1878-79 in which Azcárate did not so much summarize the debate which had taken place in the Ateneo in 1877-79, as provide a critique of different schools of thought. For a more general study of Krausist social reformism see Elías Díaz *(2)*. Galdós's treatment of the religious question in the novels of this period shows a familiarity with Azcárate's work: see Juan López Morillas, 'Galdós y el krausismo: *La familia de León Roch*', *Revista de Occidente*, 2nd series, 4 (1968), 331-57, and Aparici Llanas *(10*, pp.140-65). See also José Luis Gómez Martínez, 'Galdós y el krausismo español', *Nueva Revista de Filología Hispánica*, 32 (1983), 55-79.

tionalist position which he regarded as inadequate. He criticized the narrow view of charity held by many conservatives and advocated a return to the Pauline concept of charity as love, a concept which is present not only in *Marianela* but also in Galdós's later novels, especially *Misericordia*. Thus Azcárate, like Galdós, asserts that affection, kindness and consideration are more important than material charity, and often appreciated more than the latter by the poor themselves (*Resumen*, pp. 83-84). Although he believed the poor could do something to help themselves, his principal concern was to instil in the rich a sense of their responsibilities to the poor. The landowner of *Minuta de un testamento* urges his son, in terms reminiscent of those used by Galdós in his discussion of Nela's rights according to 'jurisprudencia cristiana' (IV, 716), to provide aid over and above what those in need are entitled to by 'justicia legal' (*Minuta*, p. 148). This reformism, as Elías Días (*2*, p. 64) points out, did not attempt to question the legitimacy of private property but idealistically attempted to bring it into harmony with the common good. Wealth was thus conceived of as having a social function and the rich man was warned not to 'encerrar sus miradas y cuidados en la esfera de su familia' but to 'tener presente los deberes que imponen la amistad, la patria, la humanidad' (*Minuta*, p. 119). Sofía and both the Penáguilas brothers are explicitly or implicitly criticized for failing to fulfil those duties.

The Krausists' demand for ethical reform was complemented by a strong emphasis on education, which was regarded as a prerequisite for lasting social reform and as indispensable for each individual to develop his or her own potential. Azcárte insists: 'no basta[...] reparar la injusticia, y remediar la miseria, sino que es preciso disipar la ignorancia, desarraigar el vicio y matar la impiedad y la superstición' (*EES*, pp. 140-41). Hence the Krausists strongly supported the introduction of free obligatory primary instruction. Although their greatest achievement in education was the creation of the Institución Libre de Enseñanza, founded to train a new intellectual elite, they were also involved, especially in the early years of the revolutionary *sexenio*, in a variety of schemes for popular education.[31]

[31]Fernando de Castro, Rector of the University of Madrid, a man much admired by Galdós, was particularly active in this field. Two organizations which owed much to his initiative were the Asociación para la Enseñanza Popular, established in 1869 to set up schools for poor children, and the

My purpose in pointing to the similarities between Galdós's view on the social question and that of the Krausists, especially as expounded by Azcárate, has not been to propose the latter's work as a source for *Marianela*, but to indicate that Galdós's position, however limited it may seem to the modern reader, was progressive for his day. The very fact that he should treat the subject at all was significant since many even denied its existence. It was, Azcárate said, necessary to 'contentarse con *afirmar* el problema social, haciendo penetrar la verdad y la realidad de los dolores de ciertas clases en la conciencia y en el corazón de aquellos que aún se obstinan en considerarlos como pura creación de imaginaciones calurientas' (*EES*, p. 137). This is precisely what Galdós has attempted to do.

Asociación para la Enseñanza de la Mujer, created in 1870 to promote women's education. Individual Krausists also gave their help to other organizations devoted to popular education: many, for example, taught at the Fomento de las Artes where several of the leading anarchists were educated.

4 *Romantic Realism*

All Galdós's 'novelas de la primera época' reveal the influence of romanticism and of the post-romantic popular novel, but none more than *Marianela*. It was, as Rafael Altamira affirmed, 'el cuadro más romántico en su asunto que Galdós ha dibujado'.[32] The literary sources which have been claimed for the novel indicate Galdós's debt to romanticism: apart from Goethe's *Wilhelm Meister*, the other works most frequently suggested belong to the tradition of social romanticism of writers such as Victor Hugo, Eugène Sue, Wenceslao Ayguals de Izco or other popular sensationalist writers such as Charles Nodier and Wilkie Collins. Moreover, the humanitarian strain of romanticism with its concern for the underdog had also been absorbed by the two realist writers whom Galdós most admired at this period and who had most influenced his work — Dickens and Balzac. Both employed the techniques of the popular novel in combination with those of realism and have been aptly described as romantic realists rather than pure realists. The essence of realism, as Tzvetan Todorov argues, is that it seeks to persuade the reader that he is dealing with a discourse whose only rule is to transcribe the real scrupulously; its one rule is to conceal all rules, to give the impression that the discourse itself is perfectly transparent, non-existent and that the reader is in direct   contact with a slice of life.[33] Whereas the realist attempts to efface his presence in order to create an illusion of reality, the romantic realist betrays his not only in direct address and exhortation to the reader but in his obvious manipulation of the narrative. In *Marianela* Galdós employs the formula of romantic realism: he combines techniques characteristic

[32]'El realismo y la literatura contemporánea', *La Ilustración Ibérica*, 4 (1886), 550-55 (p. 551). One of a series of 21 articles published between April and October 1886.

[33]'Présentation', in R. Barthes, L. Bersani, Ph. Hamon, M. Riffaterre, I. Watt, *Littérature et réalité* (Paris: Éditions du Seuil, 1982), pp. 7-10. For romantic realism in general see Donald Fanger, *Dostoevsky and Romantic Realism: A Study of Dostoevsky in Relation to Balzac, Dickens, and Gogol* (Chicago: University of Chicago Press, Phoenix Books, 1967), Chapter 1; and in relation to Galdós: Rodolfo Cardona (*13*).

of romantic and post-romantic fiction — the heightening of character, situation and pace, the exploitation of atmosphere, suspense, coincidence and extreme contrasts, and an open appeal to the readers' sentiments — with a circumstantial realism of topography, physical ambiance, dress, custom etc. The narrative discourse — the way he presents events — thus exploits the rich romantic potential of the basic story.

Structure, Plot and Setting

The overall structure of *Marianela* is climactic: there is a gradual increase in tension engineered by a progressive narrowing of options, intensive foreshadowing and the careful manipulation of time and pace. The plot is based on the principle of suspense: enigmas are posed, formulated and gradually resolved.[34] The central enigma which dominates the first fifteen chapters is whether Teodoro can give Pablo sight. In the early stages there are several options: Teodoro may examine Pablo, decide his case is hopeless and not attempt to operate; he may operate and be unsuccessful; or he may operate and be successful. At first success seems remote: blind from birth, Pablo cannot even conceive of the possibility of possessing sight (II, 705) and is convinced that his case is hopeless (II, 708). Teodoro, however, offers him a slight hope: 'Dios es inmensamente grande y misericordioso [...] ¡Quién sabe, quién sabe, amigo mío! ... Se han visto, se ven todos los días casos muy raros' (II, 708). In answer to Nela's exclamation that it is impossible that Pablo should see Teodoro says 'imposible no; aunque difícil', but concedes that Pablo may be right when he affirms that Teodoro cannot give him 'lo que la Virgen Santísima le negó desde el nacer' (III, 711). Our expectation that Pablo will see is gradually strengthened: in chapter VIII we discover that Teodoro has examined Pablo and decided to operate, giving him hope, although 'muy poca' (726), and what we learn about Teodoro in chapters IX and X — his determination, professional commitment and international reputation — lead us to anticipate his success. Teodoro himself, however, remains circumspect and warns that Pablo may undergo a painful operation and yet

---

[34]For the use of enigmas as a structuring force see Roland Barthes, *S/Z* (Paris: Éditions du Seuil, 1970).

remain blind (XI, 739). All he will say is that 'no encuentro motivos suficientes para decir: "No tiene cura", como han dicho los médicos famosos a quienes ha consultado nuestro amigo' (XI, 739) – a statement which replaced the earlier, less suspenseful version: 'hay 95 probabilidades de que vea contra 5 de que no vea' (Manuscript, p.198). Suspense reaches a peak in chapter XVI which begins with a description of the operation and concludes with the report of its success.

With the resolution of the first enigma, the narrative focuses exclusively on the question of how the new situation will affect Pablo's relationship with Nela: will it stay the same, improve or deteriorate? In effect we already know the answer for *Marianela*, unlike the popular novel, creates suspense but not surprise. Characterized by the 'irremediable fatality of Greek tragedy' (*26*, II, p. 97), the novel follows a pattern of narrowing possibilities in which the choices become more and more limited until the final choice seems no choice at all but an inevitability. The reader's attention is thus focused less on what will happen than on the implications of what happens. The foreshadowing of the tragic conclusion begins as soon as the idyllic relationship between Nela and Pablo is evoked in chapters VI-VIII. The mood moves swiftly from light-hearted optimism to dark foreboding, as Pablo's declarations of love, his vision of their future together and his passionate conviction of Nela's beauty are all systematically undercut by Nela's distraught recognition of her ugliness. Nela foresees her own despair and death when she tells Pablo 'el corazón me dice que me verás . . . ; pero me lo dice partiéndoseme', and hears her mother calling her from la Trascava (VIII, 728-29). The premonition that their relationship is doomed is reinforced by the discussion in chapter XI between Teodoro and don Francisco as to how sight will correct Pablo's distorted vision of the world, especially his contention that Nela is beautiful. The new plot option of a possible marriage between Pablo and his cousin, the dazzlingly beautiful Florentina who appears in chapter XIV, is another unequivocal pointer to catastrophe. Chapter XV contains dense foreshadowing: the title, 'Los tres', indicates a rupture in the intimacy between Nela and Pablo which is confirmed by Florentina's frequent allusions to her forthcoming marriage and her promise of patronage for Nela, the 'huerfanilla'. It ends with a sharp contrast between

Nela's instense grief at what she knows will be her fate and Pablo's continued affirmation that she is the only woman for him. From this point the action moves rapidly to the inevitable conclusion.

The climactic structure of the novel is reinforced by Galdós's manipulation of time and narrative pace. The action, excluding the events of the final chapter, is concentrated into a short space of time: it begins some time in the latter part of a September in the 1860s (II, 709) and concludes on 12 October – the date on Nela's tombstone. In these three weeks a great deal happens: Teodoro arrives, examines Pablo and decides to operate; Pablo asks Nela to marry him; Florentina and her father arrive; Teodoro operates; Pablo gains his sight and falls in love with Florentina; Nela flees and attempts suicide but is saved, brought back to Aldeacorba and then dies. Most of these events are compressed into the last third of the novel, with chapters I-XV covering one week and chapters XVI-XXI more than a fortnight. The pace in the early chapters is slowed down by extensive descriptive passages and by the introduction in flashbacks of much expository material – information about characters and the situation before the beginning of the action. In chapters I-XV time is carefully plotted day by day: chapters I-IV cover a Tuesday evening; chapters V-VII Wednesday; chapter VIII Thursday; chapter IX summarizes Teodoro's activities in the preceeding days and brings us to 'una tarde – a últimos de setiembre y seis días después de la llegada de Teodoro a las minas' (IX, 731). This day occupies chapters IX-XIII, which focus first on Teodoro and the Penáguilas (IX-XI) and then on Felipe and Nela (XII-XIII). Chapters XIV and XV cover the following day and recount the arrival of don Manuel and Florentina and the walk she takes with Pablo and Nela. From this point on, Galdós leaps over periods when little or nothing happens focusing on days when significant events occur. As a result the narrative pace quickens, tension rises and the dramatic significance of events is heightened. Thus, chapter XVI opens: 'en los días siguientes no pasó nada; mas vino uno en el cual ocurrió un hecho asombroso, capital, culminante' (750). This chapter is one of the shortest but, with the exception of the epilogue, it covers the longest period of time: it begins with an account of the operation and ends eight days later when the bandages are removed. Chapter XVII, which opens with an account of Nela's

immediate reactions, takes another leap: 'tres días más estuvo la
Nela fugitiva' (753). On the fourth day she meets and escapes from
Florentina, and this fourth day and night occupy the latter part of
chapter XVII and chapters XVIII and XIX which culminate with her
attempted suicide and rescue by Teodoro. Chapter XX flashes back
to the day the bandages were first lifted and traces Pablo's evolution
to the day Nela is brought to Aldeacorba by Teodoro. Chapter XXI
recounts Nela's death on the following day: 'fue aquel día tempe-
stuoso (y decimos aquel día, porque no sabemos qué día era: sólo
sabemos que era un día)' (767). This claim of ignorance is a means
of creating dramatic effect since we know it was October 12. The
last chapter describes, from a perspective of several months later, the
funeral, the erection of the tombstone and the subsequent newspaper report which appeared in *The Times*.

The intensification of narrative pace after chapter XV is
accompanied by a rapid narrowing of plot options. Sofía reports the
success of the operation and announces the forthcoming marriage:
'ya es cosa hecha que Pablo se casará con su prima. Buena pareja, los
dos son guapos chicos' (XVI, 751). In chapter XVII Florentina confirms that she and Pablo will be 'como uno solo', promises Nela their
protection, and informs her of Pablo's horror of the ugly, enthusiasm for the beautiful and admiration for herself (754). Nela is left
with two alternatives – 'huiré con Celipín, o me iré con mi madre'
(XVII, 752) – both of which, as Casalduero points out (*28*, p. 183,
note 1) are ambiguously evoked by the title of the next chapter: 'La
Nela se decide a partir'. The reader is initially misled into believing
that Nela will escape with Felipe, a possibility prepared for in chapters XII and XVI, but this option is soon closed and the narrative
tension increases dramatically as suicide becomes the only alter-
native. Suspense builds up rapidly: will Choto succeed in getting
Teodoro to follow him? Will Teodoro arrive in time to save Nela?
Will Nela obey Teodoro and return from la Trascava?

The tension momentarily released at the end of chapter XVIII
when Teodoro seizes hold of Nela's hand slowly begins to build up
again as the story progresses inexorably to the long-expected
dénouement. The title of chapter XIX, 'Domesticación', is deceptive
for although Teodoro temporarily succeeds in bringing Nela under
his control, the description of her as a 'cuerpo muerto' and 'marchita

como una planta que acaba de ser arrancada del suelo, dejando en él las raíces' (763) clearly foreshadows her death. Suspense is maintained by the shift in focus to Pablo in chapter XX but his obsession with physical beauty and the gradual transference of his affections from Nela to Florentina merely lead the reader by another route to the inevitable ending. The two threads of the story are brought together in chapter XXI, by far the longest in the novel, whose title, 'Los ojos matan', leaves no room for doubt as to the outcome. It opens on a relatively tranquil note as Nela sleeps, Florentina and her father discuss her charitable activities and Teodoro explains his views on Nela. The mood changes dramatically as Pablo is heard approaching: 'María se quedó lívida; alargó su cuello, sus ojos se desencajaron. Su oído prestaba atención a un ruido terrible. Había sentido pasos' (770). From this point on tension increases rapidly and the demand for our compassion becomes irresistible as we see Nela forced to hear Pablo refer to her as a 'monstruo' and passionately declare his love for Florentina. Nela is at her very ugliest when Pablo, ignorant of her identity, sees her for the first time: 'parecía que la nariz de la Nela se había hecho más picuda, sus ojos más chicos, su boca más insignificante, su tez más pecosa, sus cabellos más ralos, su frente más angosta' (XXI, 771). Such is her suffering that she seems to look at him from the depth of a sepulchre. The narrator emphasizes the drama of the moment when she touches him and he finally recognizes her: 'hubo una pausa angustiosa, una de esas pausas que preceden a las catástrofes, como para hacerlas más solemnes' (772). The inevitable catastrophe ensues and every ounce of emotion is extracted from the scene which borders on the melodramatic. This climax is possibly the most romantic of all the scenes in the novel, yet it must be remembered that the novel ends on the more positive and ironic note of the final chapter which will be discussed later.

Although the rural and industrial settings of the novel are inspired by the mines and countryside of the Santander region, their principal function is poetic: they serve less to anchor the story in reality than to comment on theme (see pp. 26-34, above), heighten character, create a mood or enhance the dramatic potential of the narrative.[35] For example, despite the use of scientific terminology to

[35]Galdós uses setting for similar purposes in his novels of the 1880s but in a much less obviously manipulative way. See William R. Risley, 'Setting in the Galdós Novel, 1881-1885', *Hispanic Review*, 46 (1978), 23-40.

describe the minerals which form the different strata of rocks in the description of the mines in chapter V, a technique reminiscent of the documentary pretensions of naturalism, the use of metaphorical language converts the mine into a living being which screams, gnashes its teeth, bites, wails, stamps, twists and grimaces. Similarly, la Terrible, as Montesinos (*24*, I, p. 243) points out, seen at moonlight permits Galdós to be 'realista y fantástico a la vez' and transform the prosaic reality of the industrial landscape into poetic vision. In the strange world of the mines Galdós discovered what Dickens, Balzac and Dostoevsky found in the modern city: the raw material for mystery and a setting as exotic as that of many a romantic novel.

Marianela's affinity with romantic realism is evident also in the polarization of the two settings, which is reinforced by a careful manipulation of time of day, designed to heighten emotional atmosphere: the industrial scenes are predominantly set at night, the pastoral scenes in the daytime. Chapters VI-VIII, which evoke the idyllic romance between Nela and Pablo, are a good example of Galdós's use of setting to create mood. It is 'un día muy hermoso', the sun is shining as they exchange confidences and make mutual protestations of love against a background of chestnut and walnut trees in full leaf, abundant flowers, and a 'grandioso panorama de verdes colinas pobladas de bosques y caseríos, de praderas llanas donde pastaban con tranquilidad vagabunda centenares de reses' (VII, 722-23). By the beginning of chapter VIII, however, 'estaba encapotado el cielo y soplaba un airecillo molesto que amenazaba convertirse en vendaval' and they decide to go down to the excavations. This change in light, weather and setting heralds a shift in mood as the carefree optimism of the previous two chapters turns to foreboding about the future. Setting is also used effectively to dramatize Nela's increasing sense of hopelessness after the success of the operation. Her attempted suicide takes place at night: fleeing from Aldeacorba she goes down to la Terrible, 'cuyo pavoroso aspecto de cráter en aquella ocasión le agradaba'. She climbs on a rock and gazes at the distant lights of Aldeacorba: 'allí estaban, brillando en el borde de la mina, sobre la oscuridad del cielo y de la tierra' (XVIII, 755). From here she goes to la Trascava meeting

Felipe on the way and refusing to escape with him. La Trascava is presented from the beginning as a place of death: 'los que han entrado no han vuelto a salir', Pablo tells Teodoro (II, 707). The negative associations are progressively intensified until, no longer a mere element of setting, it becomes a pointer to tragedy: in chapter III we learn that Nela's mother committed suicide by throwing herself down la Trascava; in chapter VIII Nela warns Pablo that it is 'un lugar peligroso' and Pablo reiterates that 'el que cae en ella no puede volver a salir' (726). Although it inspires horror in Pablo, Nela finds it 'bonita', and the progressively sombre mood of this chapter culminates with Nela hearing her mother calling her from the depths of the crevice. With such obvious signposting the reader is in little doubt as to Nela's intentions when she finally makes her way there. In the scene of the attempted suicide the setting of la Trascava, described as a 'cóncavo hueco [...], sombrío y espantoso en la oscuridad de la noche', 'negra boca', 'espantosa sima', 'horrible embudo', 'tragadero' (XVIII, 757-58), is fundamental in the creation of dramatic tension.

Nevertheless, despite the extensive exploitation of those staples of the popular novel, mystery and suspense, Galdós was unwilling to allow fantasy the upper hand. From his earliest writings he had satirized the stylistic clichés of post-romanticism (*24*, I, p. 8) and in *Marianela* he often succeeds in parodying these whilst at the same time enjoying the effects they were designed to achieve. In the opening chapter, for example, he immediately captures the curiosity of the reader and creates an atmosphere of dramatic expectation by drawing on romantic commonplaces. It is a night scene, the mysterious traveller is completely lost, he can see, smell and hear nothing. So eerie is the solitude that he comments 'si yo creyera en brujas, pensaría que el destino me proporcionaba esta noche el honor de ser presentado a ellas' (I, 703). Teodoro slips imperceptibly into the role of the romantic hero: ' "si al menos pudiera conocer el sitio donde me encuentro . . . ¡Pero qué más da!" – al decir esto hizo un gesto propio del hombre esforzado que desprecia los peligros –' (I, 703). The subsequent narrative emphasizes his courage and bravery as he presses on into the black night, losing his way in the labyrinthine paths of his desolate surroundings: 'ni alma viviente, ni chimeneas humeantes, ni ruido, ni un tren que murmure a lo lejos, ni siquiera un perro que ladre' (I, 703). As he sits down to wait for the moon to come out he hears in the distance 'un quejido poético, mejor dicho melancólico canto, formado de una sola frase, cuya última cadencia se prolongaba apianándose en la forma que los músicos llamaban *morendo*, y que se apagaba al fin en el plácido silencio de la noche, sin que el oído pudiera oír su vibración postrera'. So beautiful and moving is the voice that he wonders whether he may be about to meet 'silfos, ondinas, gnomos, hadas' (I, 704). The romanticism of the scene, however, is constantly undercut by Teodoro's attitude of commonsensical, good-humoured impatience and his use of familiar language — the irreverent, anti-romantic apostrophe of the moon as 'bribona' and 'loca' and the earth as 'holgazán satélite', his dismissal of the witches etc. as 'toda la chusma emparentada con la loca de la casa' (i.e. the imagination). His appearance moreover is hardly that of the intrepid romantic hero: 'vestía el traje propio de los señores acomodados que viajan en verano, con el redondo sombrerete, que debe a su fealdad el nombre de hongo; gemelos de campo pendientes de una correa, y grueso bastón' (I, 703).

Nela's vision of Florentina as the Virgin in chapter XIII is another scene in which Galdós ironically exploits the suspense characteristic of the world of romance, teasing the reader with an apparent miracle which turns out to have a commonplace explanation. Ironically the appearance of Florentina-Virgin signals not the miraculous transformation to beauty that Nela had hoped for — such metamorphoses belong to fairy tales such as *Beauty and the Beast* and *The Frog Prince* or to the romantic novel — but a confirmation of her ugliness. It is in terms of romance that the Centenos explain Florentina's promise to take Nela away to live with her: 'no se les ocurrió sino que a la miserable huérfana abandonada le había salido algún padre rey o príncipe como se cuenta en los romances' (XVI, 750). But this is not the world of romance as the narrator implies when he presents Florentina in words which, as Otis H. Green points out (*41*, p. 133, note 2), are reminiscent of don Quixote's vision of Dulcinea: 'no ensartando perlas, no bordando rasos con menudos hilos de oro, sino cortando un vestido con patrones hechos de *Imparciales* y otros periódicos' (XXI, 767).

Characterization

In *Marianela* Galdós's method of characterization relies heavily on techniques of poetic intensification: qualities, both physical and moral, are presented at their very extreme and their exceptional nature is often underlined by reference to a cultural archetype. Pablo, for example, is described in terms of the classical ideal of beauty: 'su cara parecía de marfil, contorneada con exquisita finura; mas teniendo su tez la suavidad de una doncella, era varonil en gran manera, y no había en sus facciones parte alguna ni rasgo que no tuviese aquella perfección soberana con que fue expresada hace miles de años, el pensamiento helénico' (V, 718-19); more specifically he has a 'rostro de Antinóo', the classical paragon of beauty (52, pp. 870-71). His body 'sólido y airoso, con admirables proporciones construido era digno en todo de la sin igual cabeza que la sustentaba'. His moral and intellectual qualities are presented in equally hyperbolic terms: he has a 'portentosa luz interior, un entendimiento de primer orden' (V, 719). Such physical and moral perfection is marred only by his blindness and the contrast is once again expressed in absolute terms: 'jamás se vio incorrección más lastimosa de la naturaleza que la que el tal representaba.' He is, in short, 'al mismo tiempo divino como un ángel, hermoso como un hombre y ciego como un vegetal' (V, 719). Florentina apparently enjoys a similar combination of extraordinary physical and moral attributes which are also intensified by comparison to a cultural archetype: 'era, sí, la auténtica imagen de aquella doncella de Nazareth, cuya perfección moral han tratado de expresar por medio de la forma pictórica los artistas de dieciocho siglos, desde San Lucas hasta el presente.' Within this tradition of Christian art she resembles the 'modo rafaelesco' which is, according to the narrator, 'sobresaliente entre todos si se atiende a que en él la perfección de la belleza humana se acerca más que ningún otro recurso artístico a la expresión de la divinidad' (XIV, 745). At the other extreme is Nela who, at Florentina's side, 'parecía hecha expresamente por la naturaleza para hacer resaltar más la perfección y magistral belleza de algunas de sus obras' (XIV, 747). Although, as we have seen, some modern critics have doubts about Florentina's virtues, from the perspective of the other characters these are absolute: Nela sees Florentina's soul as 'un hermoso paraíso abierto . . . llena de pureza, de amor, de bondades, de pensamientos discretos y consoladores' (XVI, 751); for

Teodoro 'no hay otra como Florentina' (XXI, 768), and for Pablo
she is 'la imagen más hermosa de Dios' (XXI, 771). The dominating
note of Teodoro's characterization is a robustness of body and
mind: 'era un hombre de complexión recia, buena talla, ancho de
espaldas, resuelto de ademanes, firme de andadura, basto de facciones, de mirar osado y vivo, ligero a pesar de su regular obesidad, y
(dígase de una vez aunque sea prematuro), excelente persona por
doquiera que se le mirara' (I, 702); he is, in his own words, 'el
hombre más serio y menos supersticioso del mundo' (I, 703). His
strength of physique and character are emphasized by consistent
comparisons with a lion (IX, 730; XVI, 750; XVIII, 757; XIX, 759
and 762; XXI, 773) and his enterprise and achievements through
reference to the cultural archetypes of Christopher Columbus and
Hernán Cortés (X, 736).

This concentration of physical and moral qualities which is
present in minor as well as major characters tends to create types
who incarnate social and moral forces rather than individuals. We are
thus encouraged to read the novel in terms of general issues rather
than of particular, individualized relationships. In his novels of the
1880s Galdós achieves a more even balance between the general and
the particular and creates characters who live both as individuals and
as social types. The heightening of characters also tends to polarize
them into positive and negative in a way which suggests the sharp
antitheses of the popular novel. Florentina's beauty emphasizes
Nela's ugliness; the grasping meanness of the Centenos is highlighted
by contrast with the patriarchal generosity of don Francisco; Sofía's
narrow, conventional view of charity accentuates the progressive,
humane views of Teodoro; don Manuel's obsession with decorum
and material values throws into relief his daughter's spontaneity and
recognition of the importance of human values.

These romantic features of characterization are, however, bal-
anced by others which aim at verisimilitude. Galdós's presentation is
not so extreme as to defy plausibility. Although Florentina, Teodoro
and don Francisco have more than their fair share of good qualities,
and Sofía and don Manuel of bad qualities, the former are all guilty
of insensitivity and the latter are narrow in outlook rather than
deliberately wicked. Even the Centeno parents – the closest Galdós
comes to the depiction of evil – seem positively harmless when

compared to such surrogate devil figures as Balzac's Vautrin or Dickens's Fagin. Galdós's relatively realistic presentation is evident if the Centenos are compared to the Thénardier family in Hugo's *Les Misérables*, on whom it has been claimed they were closely modelled (*50*, pp. 125-29). The Thénardier couple are not merely avaricious, they are criminally corrupt, and they treat Cosette, the little girl left in their care, with a spiteful brutality far worse than the cold-hearted indifference with which the Centenos treat Nela. Futhermore, Galdós shows that the fate of the Centeno offspring is only marginally better than that of Nela, and he thus avoids Hugo's facile contrast between the suffering the Thénardier parents inflict on Cosette and the pampered treatment they lavish on their daughter, Éponine. Whereas Hugo has recourse to the gratuitous villainy of melodrama, Galdós attempts to place the vices of the Centenos in a wider sociological context. He also mutes the extremism of his portrayal of negative characters by greying their vices not with virtues but with humour, a technique characteristic of Dickens.

In *Marianela* Galdós makes extensive use of summary definition of character: the narrator presents a synthetic vision of most of the characters, summing up their past history and principal personality traits. This technique, which threatens verisimilitude by drawing attention to the manipulations of the narrator, was used less by Galdós as his style matured and he relied more on dialogue and action to present character (*15*, pp. 113-14). On several occasions, however, Galdós attempts to efface the presence of the narrator by allowing the characters to recount their own past — as is the case with Nela (III) and Teodoro (IX and X). Moreover, all three major characters, Teodoro, Pablo, and Nela, are initially presented in scenes in which information is provided in an apparently casual fashion, thus enabling readers to begin to form their own opinion before they have the benefit of the narrator's summary. Furthermore, the narrator's summary is not always reliable: the description of Sofía as 'una excelente señora' who 'había hecho prodigios, ofreciendo ejemplos dignos de imitación a todas las almas aficionadas a la caridad' (IX, 730) is obviously ironical when viewed in the light of the scene with Lilí — a good example of Galdós's ability to make effective use of scene to define character — and the discussion on the social problem with Teodoro.

Although critics disagree as to whether the characters in *Maria-nela* are convincing or merely lifeless abstractions, most regard the characterization of Nela — undoubtedly the most complex character — as a remarkable achievement. Indeed it was Galdós's analysis of her conflicting desires and emotions that led Pardo Bazán and Pereda to classify the novel as a psychological drama. Nevertheless, it is Nela's character and plight which contribute most to the romantic colouring of the novel. She belongs, like Dickens's Oliver Twist and Hugo's Cosette, to a long line of innocent, abandoned orphans, endowed with sensitivity, imagination and an affectionate heart who are the victims of a cruel and indifferent society. The pathos of her situation is further intensified by the fact that she is also created in the image of another romantic stereotype: the character whose beautiful soul is imprisoned in an ugly body. She thus has a double claim on the reader's compassion as a victim of iniquitous social conditions and as a victim of a hopeless passion — a combination which was, as Revilla pointed out, 'la forma más refinada de sufri-miento que pudo imaginar la imaginación del más implacable de los demonios'. Marianela, he argued, was not 'un personaje real sino un bello fantasma soñado por el Sr. Galdós' (*33*, pp. 505-06). Paradoxi-cally however, Marianela, the most romantic of the characters in conception, is the most realistically presented. In her characteriza-tion Galdós employs techniques used rarely with other characters; in particular he permits the reader access to her mind through narrative summary and internal monologue, thus giving us the illusion that we are closer to her. Comparison with similar literary types illustrates Galdós's concern to root the most romantic aspects of her character and conduct firmly in a psychological and social reality. The enig-matic origins of Goethe's Mignon and Dickens's Oliver Twist, for example, abound in sensationalist elements — sacrilege, incest, illegit-imacy, kidnapping, etc. — which are revealed in delayed melodrama-tic disclosures. Promiscuity, illegitimacy and suicide are present in Nela's past too but they are part of the social theme, not elements of mystery and suspense. The account of her life in the Centeno house-hold, while casting her in the role of romantic victim, also explains her desperate need for love and sense of inferiority which play such an important part in her psychological development (*16*, p. 10). Much of the lyricism of the novel is attributable to Nela's romantic role as a child of nature – her poetic interpretation of the universe, life and death, the flowers and the stars – but Galdós is at pains to explain her vision in social and psychological terms as the consequence of her social isolation and ignorance. Even at the end of the novel, where the romantic elements reach their peak with her attempted suicide and death, Galdós attempts to make them plausible by suggesting a possible pathological cause (*24*, p. 243; *26*, II p. 96).

Language

Galdós and his fellow realists were particularly conscious of the need to forge a literary language free from rhetorical excess which would foster the illusion that the novel merely mirrored reality. Referring to the problem in his prologue to Pereda's *El sabor de la tierruca* (1882) Galdós remarked: 'una de las mayores dificultades con que tropieza la novela en España consiste en lo poco hecho y trabajado que está el lenguaje literario para reproducir los matices de la conversación' (*9*, p. 166).[36] He eventually evolved a style which individualized characters through diction appropriate to their class, condition and profession, and camouflaged the fictitiousness of the narrative behind the familiarity of ordinary, everyday language. In *Marianela*, however, he was still experimenting and at times self-consciously draws attention to his efforts or lapses into an implausible affectation. For example, one of the weakest points of Nela's characterization, as Revilla (*33*, p. 508) pointed out, was that she spoke 'como una doctora'. Her solecisms are rare ('las Inglaterras': III, 711), her colloquialisms few, and on occasion she uses cultivated expressions ('no te afanes por verme': VIII, 729; 'aprendieron el modo de hacerse personas cabales': XII, 740), and phrases with an archaic flavour ('ellos con su buen gobierno se volvieron sabios': XXII, 740). Her internal monologue in chapter XIII (743) provides a good example of the improbable ease with which she employs romantic

[36]For an intelligent discussion of the problem and an assessment of Galdós's contribution to a new literary style see Leopoldo Alas, 'Del estilo en la novela' — a series of articles originally published in *Arte y Letras* in 1881-2 and reprinted in Leopoldo Alas: *Teoría y crítica de la novela españa*, ed. Sergio Beser (Barcelona: Laia, 1972), pp.51-86.

rhetoric ('que se trague la tierra mi fealdad'), a remarkably rich and
varied vocabulary ('¿cómo es posible que me quiera viendo este
cuerpo chico, esta figurilla de pájaro, esta tez pecosa, esta boca sin
gracia, esta nariz picuda, este pelo descolorido?') and rhetorical
flourishes such as the syntactical parallelism leading to a climax in
the following example: '¡si yo fuese grande y hermosa; si tuviera el
talle, la cara y el tamaño . . . , sobre todo el tamaño de otras mujeres;
si yo pudiese llegar a ser señora y componerme! . . . ¡Ay!, entonces
mi mayor delicia sería que sus ojos se recrearan en mí.' Galdós was,
nevertheless, aware of the dangers of providing Nela with a diction
inappropriate to her condition and attempted to overcome the
problem thus:

Si Marianela usara ciertas voces, habría dicho:

'Mi dignidad no me permite aceptar el atroz desaire que voy
a recibir. Puesto que Dios quiere que sufra esta humillación,
sea; pero no he de asistir a mi destronamiento; Dios bendiga a
la que por ley natural ocupará mi puesto; pero no tengo valor
para sentarla yo misma en él.'

No pudiendo hablar así, su rudeza expresaba la misma idea
de este otro modo:

'No vuelvo más a Aldeacorba . . . No consentiré que me vea
. . . Huiré con Celipín, o me iré con mi madre. Ahora yo no
sirvo para nada.' (XVII, 752)

Although Felipe occasionally displays a command of rhetoric
unusual in one so young and uneducated — as for example in his
analysis of the effect of the mines (IV, 714) — his speech is more in
accord with his social condition than that of Nela. It is characterized
by a linguistic tic ('¡Córcholis!', or in moments of great excitement
'¡Recórcholis!'), solecisms (*fantesía*: IV, 714; *miá*: XII, 740;
conceitos; echar *retólicas* XII, 741; *mesma*: XVII, 753), diminutives
(solito, Nelilla: IV, 714), colloquialisms ('debo tirar para médico';
'¡Escribir!, a mí con esas': XXII, 740-41) and syntactic simplicity,
as for example in the use of coordination rather than subordination:

Tomaremos el tren, y en el tren iremos hasta donde podamos
. . . Y después pediremos limosna hasta llegar a los Madriles del
Rey de España, tú te pondrás a servir en una casa de marqueses
y condeses, y yo en otra, y así, mientras yo estudie, tú podrás
aprender muchas finuras. (XVIII, 756)

Galdós also attempts to individualize the speech of Teodoro who
speaks 'por lo general incorrectamente por ser incapaz de construir
con gracia y elegancia las oraciones. Sus frases, rápidas y entrecorta-
das, se acomodaban a la emisión de su pensamiento, que era una
especie de emisión eléctrica' (IX, 730). Thus his account of his past
in chapter X consists of a succession of short phrases punctuated by
suspension points. Nevertheless, his language is by no means free of
rhetorical flourishes ('yo no sé qué extraordinario rayo de energía
vibró dentro de mí': X, 735) and tends to border on the grandilo-
quent, especially when he declaims on the social problem. However,
although Galdós no doubt found it difficult to shake off the custom-
ary rhetoric (*12*, pp. 209-10) employed to discuss such matters in
newspapers and academies, he was aware of the problem and, as we
have seen, draws attention to the inopportune pomposity of Teodoro's language. Another novel aspect of Teodoro's speech which
serves to characterize him professionally is his use of technical jargon
of the kind not traditionally regarded as appropriate for the novel.
The danger that he might sound foolishly affected as he addresses a
lay audience is avoided through a combination of specialized
terminology and lively, figurative language:

Su Majestad la retina se halla quizá dispuesta a recibir los rayos
lumínicos que se le quieran presentar. Su alteza el humor
vítreo probablemente no tendrá novedad. Si la larguísima falta
de ejercicio en sus funciones le ha producido algo de glaucoma
. . . , una especie de tristeza . . . , ya trataremos de arreglarlo.
Todo estará bien allá en la cámara regia. (XI, 739)

Teodoro's language is the most interesting in that it illustrates
most clearly Galdós's attempts to forge a conversational style. The
language of other characters, except for Felipe, is less original,
either because they have longer literary pedigrees or because their

personalities demand a rather more stilted discourse. Florentina belongs to a tradition of girlish romantic heroines and speaks with the coy innocence regarded as highly attractive in these exemplars of femininity, as for example in her frequent euphemistic allusions to her forthcoming marriage or her ingenuous comments on the unequal distribution of wealth: ' es cosa que no comprendo . . . ¡Que algunos tengan tanto y otros tan poco! . . . Me enfado con papá cuando le oigo decir palabrotas contra los que quieran que se reparta por igual todo lo que hay en el mundo. ¿Cómo se llaman estos tipos Pablo?' (XV, 748). Sofía and don Manuel employ a language suited to their pompous and self-important personalities. The latter's habit of repeating his last phrases, which is commented upon by the narrator (XIV, 746), is used also for comic effect (*28*, p. 161, n. 8). Pablo's speech is the most mannered and rhetorical, the furthest from the familiar conversational style Galdós was attempting to elaborate, but the romantic grandiloquence is of course deliberate: it reveals his passionate and exalted nature, and his tendency to see things in extremes. The change he undergoes on gaining his sight is subtly indicated by the fact that he unconsciously begins to mimic his uncle's linguistic tic − 'hay que protegerla, Florentina; protegerla'; 'esto no se puede sufrir; no, no se puede sufrir . . . ' (XX, 766).

In 1897 in the prologue to *El abuelo* Galdós extolled the virtues of dialogue as a means of creating an illusion of reality and allowing us to forget the hidden artist (*9*, pp. 205-07). In *Marianela*, however, as in the other early novels, the abundance of dialogue illustrates Galdós's fondness for the theatre rather than a desire for objectivity. Thus, although much of the story is carried forward through dialogue, this rarely operates independently of the narrator's explicit or implicit comment: his point of view dominates all the presented material.

The Narrator

From the moment the narrator addresses the reader in the opening paragraph − 'ya se ve que estamos en el Norte de España' (I, 702) − we are constantly aware of his presence. Despite an occasional confession of ignorance or uncertainty ('parecía impaciente', I, 52; 'no sabemos qué día era', XXI, 767), he has the characteristic powers of an omniscient narrator: he provides information about the past, enters the minds of his characters and summarizes character, time and space. Such abilities generally do little to impair the illusion of reality since they belong to the literary conventions readily accepted by the reader. His frequent intrusions to comment on his own narrative procedures, however, generally betray an awkwardness in making a smooth transition from one point of view or point in time to another, or an uneasy need to justify some aspect of the narrative as in the following examples: 'hemos descrito el trato que tenían en caso de Centeno los hijos, para que se comprenda el que tendría la Nela' (IV, 716); 'la Nela cerró sus conchas para estar más sola. Sigámosla; penetremos en su pensamiento. Pero antes conviene hacer algo de historia' (XIII, 742). Elsewhere he indicates that he has selected his material and decided what is worth telling and what not: he chooses to relay only certain parts of Nela's prayer to the Virgin, 'que si se escribiera habría de ser curiosa' (XIV, 744), and only part of the conversation between Florentina, Pablo and Nela: 'hablaron algo más; pero después de lo que se consigna, nada de cuanto dijeron es digno de ser transmitido al lector' (XV, 750). At times he is less certain: he wonders whether the conversation between Nela and Teodoro is worth a separate chapter and adds: 'por si acaso se lo daremos' (II, 709). Sometimes he draws attention to the narrative process by admitting to his own technical limitations – 'es absolutamente imposible describir los sentimientos de la vagabunda' (XVI, 751) – or by commenting on what characters did not say or think, as for example when he interprets Lili's expression as disdain for Sofía or when he speculates on how Marianela might have expressed herself had she a command of cultivated diction (XVII, 752).

The narrator also advertises his presence when he seeks to relate his characters and their situations to the real world. His commentary is not restricted to unobtrusive generalizations which can often foster an illusion of reality by combining fictional happenings with widely accepted assumptions about the world – for example his assertion that love and affection are more important than a few scraps of food (IV, 716) or that the vanity of the self-made man is excusable (IX, 730) – but, as we have seen, often takes the form of lengthy disquisitions. The fact that much of the commentary is handed over to Teodoro is not necessarily any less damaging to plausibility and the overt didacticism of the novel is yet another feature which approximates it to romantic rather than pure realism.

Despite the fact that Galdós's use of the narrator in *Marianela* at times contravenes the principal aim of literary realism — to create the illusion that the reader is in direct contact with unmediated reality — it is largely through the narrator that he seeks to impose the realistic vision of life which was associated with literary realism. Although the narrator is not dramatized as a character, there is sufficient information about him to enable the reader to form a picture of him as an educated and cultivated man (indicated by his allusions to Greek and Christian art) of the middle class. His commentary consistently echoes the attitudes and views of Teodoro: he shares the latter's admiration for the wonders of science and his conviction that there are mysteries science can never penetrate (XVI, 750). Like Teodoro, he is a rationalist who refuses to believe in supernatural apparitions: he dismisses Nela's belief that she sees the Virgin as 'pueril candor' (XVI, 751). His analysis of Nela's psychology and situation coincides with that of Teodoro and he shares the latter's concern and sympathy for her. Intellectually, though not emotionally, the narrator is distant from those characters who are the source of most of the romantic and lyrical elements in the novel — Pablo and Nela — and his commentary provides a realist corrective to their idealistic vision. For example, the exalted and passionate mood of chapters VI-VIII is created through the extensive use of dialogue with narrative commentary cut to a minimum. Pablo articulates the clichés of romantic love: that he and Nela were predestined for each other and each is incomplete without the other; that she is endowed with a divine moral and physical perfection; that he feels for her 'un amor grande, insaciable, eterno'; that he would be satisfied to see her only for one day; that he would rather remain blind than lose her and would die if she did not love him and finally that their love will transcend all social barriers. The reader is never in much doubt that such a romantic passion is doomed to pass: the implicit appeal to our knowledge of the world — that rich, handsome young men rarely marry poor, ugly young women — is reinforced by the narrator's explicit comments on the unrealistic nature of the characters' view of the relationship: Pablo is 'llevado de su ardiente fantasía', 'arrastrado al absurdo por su delirante entendimiento' (VII, 725), and Nela talks 'con desvarío' (VIII, 729). There is no evidence to suggest that the values and assumptions of the narrator are in any way opposed to those of the implied author.[37] In Galdós's novels and in the realist novel in general, as Engler points out, 'the distance between the implied author and the narrator, intellectually, morally, ethically and psychologically, is virtually nil' (*15*, p. 102). Moreover, the narrator of *Marianela* also addresses himself to an implied reader who shares his own cultural, intellectual and social assumptions: like most nineteenth-century novels 'it is told from the viewpoint of wisdom and experience and listened to from the viewpoint of order'.[38]

---

[37]The implied author is not the flesh-and-bones, real author but the author as reconstructed by the reader from the narrative. He is, as Wayne C. Booth points out, an ideal, literary, created version of the real author and is sometimes referred to as the 'official scribe' or the 'author's second self'. See Wayne C. Booth, *The Rhetoric of Fiction*, 2nd ed. (Chicago: University of Chicago Press, 1983), pp.71-76.

[38]Jonathan Culler, *Structuralist Poetics: Structuralism, Linguistics and the Study of Literature* (London: Routledge and Kegan Paul, 1975, p.195). Culler is summarizing Jean-Paul Sartre, *Qu'est-ce que la littérature?* (Paris: Gallimard, 1948), pp.172-73.

5 Conclusion

Although Galdós had made clear his commitment to a non-didactic realist novel as early as 1870, it was not until the 1880s that the programme outlined in his 'Observaciones sobre la novela contemporánea en España' began to be fully realized. His 'novelas de la primera época' betray the influence of literary Idealism — which embraced romanticism — in their abstract and imaginary settings, their tendency to subordinate character and plot to a previously conceived ideological scheme, and their overt didacticism. The romantic composition and conspicuous symbolism of *Marianela* make it possibly the most idealist in conception of these early novels — Galdós himself apparently dismissed it as 'una debilidad de la fantasía, un homenaje al idealismo trasnochado'.[39] But despite this debt to Idealism, the novel not only dramatizes the conflict between ideals and illusions and the facts of real life which is at the core of most realist novels (*14*, pp. 36-37), it presents a defence of the realist aesthetic as the most appropriate for exploring the ills of contemporary society. That literature should retain close contact with the real world if it were to contribute to progress was a notion which, as Rodgers (*25*, p. 243) has demonstrated, Galdós derived from Krausist aesthetics.

Galdós's case for realism is put most clearly and wittily in the final chapter, '¡Adiós!', a *tour de force* which draws together the social, philosophical and aesthetic implications of the story. Had he been writing a romantic novel, undoubtedly he would have ended with the harrowing account of the heroine's death. However, though he wished his readers to react sympathetically to the pathos of Nela's plight, he was clearly determined to avoid the facile sentimentalism which might do little more than afford the reader the satisfaction of a good cry. He therefore distances the reader from the events of the story both in time and through the narrator's perspective of ironic detachment. The latter's commentary on the ironic contrast between Nela's deprivation in life and the gifts

[39]Leopoldo Alas, *Teoría y crítica de la novela española*, p.83.

lavished on her in death — a funeral and tomb so magnificent they arouse the admiration and envy of the living — focuses the reader's attention on the social message by implicitly criticizing those who did nothing for her whilst she was alive (*28*, p. 229, note 1). It also illustrates the futility of mere material remedies.

In the second part of the chapter, which recounts the version of Nela's life supposedly concocted several months later by some English tourists and printed in *The Times* under the title *Sketches from Cantabria*, the reader is distanced from the story even further. This account transforms Nela into a wealthy aristocratic young lady, Doña Mariquita Manuela Téllez, whose whim it was to dress in rags 'para confundirse con la turba de mendigos, buscones, trovadores, frailes, hidalgos, gitanos y muleteros, que en *las kermesas* forman esa abigarrada plebe española que subsiste y subsistirá siempre, independiente y pintoresca, a pesar de los *rails* y de los periódicos que han empezado a introducirse en la Península Occidental' (XXII, 775). She is, they claim, a young lady to whom numerous ballads, sonnets and madrigals have been dedicated by Spanish poets. The narrator offers his own account as a realist corrective to this extravagant tale: 'bastaba leer esto para comprender que los dignos reporteros habían visto visiones. Averiguado la verdad, de ello resultó este libro' (XXII, 775; cf. the insistence on the truth of his story in IX, 730, and XXII, 774). The condemnation of the lies of literature is of course a commonplace device employed by novelists to suggest that their own work is a privileged exception, an accurate, undistorted account of what really happened. The introduction of the *Sketches from Cantabria* version, however, not only establishes the truth of the narrator's version of events, it also provides a comment on the central themes of the novel. The fact that the tourists' account is a product of their misinterpretation of visible evidence — they write it as a result of seeing Nela's magnificent tomb — reaffirms the theme of the deceptiveness of appearances and could be taken to indicate, as Wellington suggests, a lack of faith in the positivist method of observation as an exclusive guide to truth (*53*, p. 46). The tomb, however, is merely a starting-point. The account is based on conventional preconceptions most of which derive from literature: it fits in with a picturesque and picaresque vision of a romantic Spain, barely touched by modern civilization, which the tourists from England —

at that time at the forefront of industrial and material progress —
can afford to contemplate with complacent condescension. By
making the English women the butt of his irony, Galdós implicitly
condemns the inadequacy of this nostalgic, backward-looking view
which, ignorant of the real conditions of the 'plebe española',
portrays them in an idealized, distorted way. Possibly, as Casalduero
(*28*, p. 229, note 1) suggests, Galdós also intended to satirize the
popular novel whose impoverished heroines were wont to turn out
to be aristocratic heiresses.

Galdós also defends the realist aesthetic in other aspects of
Marianela which implicitly raise issues central to the contemporary
debate between Idealism and Realism. Realism was frequently
charged with a failure to exercise artistic selection in its obsessive
concern with material reality; it concentrated, it was claimed, on the
vulgar, the prosaic and the ugly and excluded lofty ideals, noble
sentiments and the beautiful. Galdós, in his perception of the epic
grandeur of industry and of the noble and heroic qualities of the
bluff, bowler-hatted ophthalmologist, demonstrates that like Alas he
believed that 'si de toda la realidad se puede hacer asunto de novela
no es porque se haya descubierto que la novela puede ser prosaica,
sino porque en toda realidad se puede ver poesía'.[40] That the creation of beauty should be one, if not the only, function of art was a
point on which most participants in the debate agreed but defini-
tions of what constituted the beautiful differed. Luis Vidart identified three basic positions: Materialism which identified beauty with
an exact reproduction of the material world, Idealism which identified it with 'la fantasía, creyendo que la obra literaria será tanto más
bella, cuanto más se aparte de la realidad de la vida', and Realism
'que busca la belleza en la realidad entera de la vida, en ese drama
interno-externo que eternamente se representa en la conciencia de la
humanidad'.[41] The critical portrayal of Pablo's evolution from an

[40]Leopoldo Alas, *Teoría y crítica de la novela española*, p.284. In the debates on
realism held in the Ateneo de Madrid in 1875 Manuel de la Revilla argued that
realism would present no threat to modern art, nor would it lack 'inspiración y
grandeza', provided artists took inspiration from 'los grandes descubrimientos
de la ciencia, las maravillas de la industria, la grandiosa epopeya revolucionaria
que se va desarrollando desde 89 acá, la idea del progreso, única fé y única
esperanza del siglo XIX', 'El realismo en el arte dramático' cited in one of a
series of summaries of the debates which appeared in the *Revista Europea*, 4
(1875), 115-19. 194-99, 273-74, 318-20, 400, 475-79 (quotation from p.199).

[41]'El realismo en el arte dramático', *Revista Europea*, 4 (1875), 273-74, (p.273).
For Galdós's views see Ned J. Davison 'Galdós's Conception of Beauty, Truth
and Reality in Art', *Hispania* (U.S.A.), 38 (1955), 52-54.

idealist to a materialist concept of beauty and the vindication of the beauty of Nela's soul indicate that, rather than an allegorical representation of Galdós's rejection of fantasy (the death of Marianela) in favour of 'la realidad captada por los sentidos' as Casalduero suggests (*12*, p. 220), the novel expresses a commitment to the realist concept of beauty which embraced both matter and spirit. Galdós's concept of realism was never limited to mere mimesis, or imitation of external reality, but was based on a profound awareness that realism was a product of the interplay between external reality and the perceiving consciousness (*13*; *15*, pp. 43-44). Time and again the novel implicitly reminds the reader that all views of reality are ultimately subjective: through the contrast between the scientific and the imaginative descriptions of the mines, through the conflicting attitudes of different characters to Nela and finally, but most effectively, through Teodoro's realization that 'la realidad ha sido para él nueva vida; para ella ha sido [...] ¡la muerte!' (XXI, 773).

Marianela, as both Beyrie and Casalduero point out (*11*, II, p. 298; *12*, p. 220), marked a turning-point in Galdós's work: though in many ways romantic in conception, it nevertheless points to a concept of the novel closer to the notion of pure realism which he was to adopt in his novels of the 1880s and 1890s. Current fashions for objectivity and ambiguity perhaps make the latter more acceptable to modern taste but the aesthetic formula Galdós adopted in *Marianela* has been undeniably most successful, as the novel's enduring popularity demonstrates. This novel also has much to offer the serious student of Galdós: it both captures the ideological and aesthetic preoccupations of the novelist and his society in the post-revolutionary period of transition, and expresses concerns and attitudes (for example, on education, charity, the need to harmonize the material and the spiritual), many of which owed much to Krausism, that were to persist throughout Galdós's work.

Bibliographical Note

A. BIBLIOGRAPHIES

For details of the editions of Galdós's works see Miguel Hernández Suárez, *Bibliografía de Galdós*, I (Las Palmas: Excmo. Cabildo Insular, 1972).

For further critical guidance see Theodore A. Sackett, *Pérez Galdós: An Annotated Bibliography* (Albuquerque: University of New Mexico Press, 1968); Hensley C. Woodbridge, *Benito Pérez Galdós: A Selective Annotated Bibliography* (Metuchen, NJ: Scarecrow Press, 1975) and *Benito Pérez Galdós: an Annotated Bibliography for 1975-1980* (1981) (reproduced in xerox and microfilm by General Microfilm Company, Massachusetts); J.E. Varey, 'Galdós in the light of recent criticism', in *Galdós Studies*, ed. J.E. Varey (London: Tamesis, 1970), pp.1-35; Anthony Percival, *Galdós and his Critics* (Toronto: University Press, 1985).

B. HISTORICAL AND IDEOLOGICAL BACKGROUND

1. Raymond Carr, *Spain 1808-1939* (Oxford: Clarendon Press, 1966). The standard general study of the period.
2. Elías Díaz, *La filosofía social del krausismo español* (Madrid: Cuadernos para el Diálogo, 1973). Good introduction to Krausist social philosophy.
3. C.A.M. Hennessey, *The Federal Republic in Spain: Pi y Margall and the Federal Republican Movement (1868-1874)* (Oxford: Clarendon Press, 1962). Excellent guide to the period, especially to the politics of the left.
4. Clara Lida and Iris Zavala (ed.), *La revolución de 1868: historia, pensamiento, literatura* (New York: Las Américas, 1970). Useful collection of essays.
5. Juan López Morillas, *El krausismo español*, 2nd ed. (México: Fondo de Cultura Económica, 1980). A good general study of Krausism.
6. Diego Núñez Ruiz, *La mentalidad positiva en España: desarrollo y crisis* (Madrid: Tucar, 1975). Best account of influence of positivism.

C. BIOGRAPHIES

7. H. Chonon Berkowitz, *Benito Pérez Galdós: Spanish Liberal Crusader* (Madison: University of Wisconsin Press, 1948). Dated; does not give sources but still useful.
8. Benito Madariaga & Celia Valbuena de Madariaga, *Pérez Galdós: biografía santanderina; cronología, producción literaria y estrenos teatrales en Santander* (Santander: Institución Cultural de Cantabria, Instituto de Literatura 'José María de Pereda', 1979). Very thorough study of Galdós's contacts with the Santander region. For *Marianela* see chapter XV.

D. GALDÓS ON THE NOVEL

9. Laureano Bonet (ed.), *Benito Pérez Galdós: ensayos de crítica literaria* (Barcelona: Península, 1972). Contains most important theoretical statements. Good introduction.

E. GENERAL CRITICAL WORKS

10. María Pilar Aparici Llanas, *Las novelas de tesis de Benito Pérez Galdós* (Barcelona: Consejo Superior de Investigaciones Científicas, 1982). Concentrates on *Doña Perfecta, Gloria* and *La familia de León Roch;* useful for historical and ideological background and narrative techniques.

11. Jacques Beyrie, *Galdós et son mythe,* 3 vols (Lille: Atelier Reproduction des Thèses, Université de Lille, 1980). Illuminating, comprehensive study of Galdós's early development. For *Marianela* see II, pp.283-99.

12. Joaquín Casalduero, *Vida y obra de Benito Pérez Galdós (1843-1920),* 3rd ed. (Madrid: Gredos, 1970). Influential pioneering study, but excessively schematic interpretations. Appendix II, pp.201-03, reprints '*Marianela y De l'intelligence* de Taine', PMLA, 50 (1935), 929-31, which claims Taine as a source. Appendix III, 204-36 reprints 'Auguste Comte y *Marianela',* Smith College Studies in Modern Languages, 21 (1939), 10-25, -- a controversial symbolical interpretation of the novel as an endorsement of Comtian positivism.

13. Rodolfo Cardona, 'Galdós and Realism', in *Galdós (Papers Read at the Modern Foreign Language Department Symposium: Nineteenth-Century Spanish Literature: Benito Pérez Galdós)* (Fredericksburg, Virginia: Mary Washington College of the University of Virginia, 1967), pp.71-94. Stimulating discussion of Galdós's realism.

14. Gustavo Correa, *Realidad, ficción y símbolo en las novelas de Pérez Galdós: ensayo de estética realista* (Bogotá: Instituto Caro y Cuervo, 1967). Useful contribution to the topic.

15. Kay Engler, *The Structure of Realism: The 'Novelas contemporáneas' of Benito Pérez Galdós,* University of North Carolina Studies in the Romance Languages and Literatures, 184 (Chapel Hill: University of North Carolina Press, 1977). Important study which concentrates on novels of the 1880s.

16. Sherman H. Eoff, *The Novels of Pérez Galdós: The Concept of Life as Dynamic Process* (Saint Louis. Washington University Studies, 1954). Concentrates on psychological and philosophical aspects. Can still be read with profit.

17. Gerald Gillespie, 'Galdós and Positivism', in *Galdós* (see *13*), pp.109-20. Brief but useful.

18. Stephen Gilman, *Galdós and the Art of the European Novel* (Princeton: University Press, 1981). Perceptive study.

19. Peter B. Goldman, 'Galdós and the Nineteenth Century Novel: The

Need for an Interdisciplinary Approach', *AG*, 10 (1975), 5-18. Makes
cogent case for the need to study Galdós's work in its historical and
social context.

20. Ricardo Gullón, *Galdós, novelista moderno*, 3rd ed. (Madrid: Gredos,
1973). Broad, rather dated study.

21. Hans Hinterhauser, *Los 'Episodios nacionales' de Benito Pérez Galdós*,
translated by José Escobar (Madrid: Gredos, 1963). Contains lucid
insights.

22. Robert Kirsner, *Veinte años de matrimonio en la novelística de Galdós*
(Eastchester, NY: Eliseo Torres, 1983). The only general study of
subject; fails to take into account much recent criticism. For
Marianela see pp.59-68.

23. Denah Lida, 'Sobre el «krausismo» de Galdós', *AG*, 2 (1967), 1-27.
General study with good bibliography.

24. José F. Montesinos, *Galdós*, 3 vols (Madrid: Castalia, 1968-73).
Rambling but often very perceptive. For *Marianela* see I, pp.235-50.

25. Eamonn Rodgers, 'El krausismo, piedra angular de la novelística de
Galdós', *Boletín de la Biblioteca de Menéndez Pelayo*, 62 (1986),
241-53. Persuasively argues that Galdós's concept of literary realism
derives from Krausist aesthetics.

26. William H. Shoemaker, *The Novelistic Art of Galdós*, 3 vols (Valencia:
Albatros, 1980-82). Solid study with much bibliographical information.
For *Marianela* see II, 86-103.

27. Diane F. Urey, *Galdós and the Irony of Language* (Cambridge:
University Press, 1982). Intelligent and stimulating although nothing
specifically on *Marianela*.

F.   EDITIONS *(see also Preface)*

28. Joaquín Casalduero (Madrid: Cátedra, 1983). The introduction is largely
based on Casalduero's earlier work on *Marianela* (see *12*) and does not
take into account subsequent criticism. Extensive footnotes.

29. María Angélica Ortega Celis, Biblioteca Escolar Literaria, 16
(Madrid: Santillana, 1975). Elementary introduction and 11-page
analysis.

30. Pascual Izquierdo, Tus Libros (Madrid: Anaya, 1982; reprinted 1983).
Based on the 4th edition published in 1882. Notes. Appendix contains a
largely irrelevant survey of historical background, brief comments on
Galdós's life and works, and an unfavourable analysis.

G.   CONTEMPORARY REVIEWS

31. Leopoldo Alas, *Galdós* (Madrid: Renacimiento, 1912), pp.63-74.
(Originally published in *El Solfeo*, 13 and 14 April 1878). A favourable
review which makes very interesting observations. Suggests Goethe's
Mignon as source.

32. Emilia Pardo Bazán, 'Estudios de literatura contemporánea: Pérez
Galdós', *Revista Europea*, 15 (1880), 347-50, 375-79, 412-13. The last

article deals with *Marianela*. Generally favourable but criticizes lack of verisimilitude and the social message.

33. Manuel de la Revilla, 'Revista crítica', *Revista Contemporánea,* 14 (1878), 505-09. Praises poetic qualities but finds some aspects implausible. Suggests as sources Goethe's Mignon (*Wilhelm Meister*), and Hugo's Quasimodo (*Notre Dame de Paris)*, Gilliat (*Les Travailleurs de la mer*), Gwymplaine and Dea (*L'Homme qui rit*).

34. Un lunático, 'Pérez Galdós, *Marianela*', *El Imparcial* (8 April 1878), p.3. (Reprinted in *La Guirnalda,* 12 (1878), 71-72). Enthusiastic.

35. Count M. Toulouse Lautrec, 'Un Romancier espagnol contemporain', *Le Correspondant* (Paris), 132 (1883), 518-43. Laudatory, descriptive review.

H.   *STUDIES OF 'MARIANELA'*

36. Louise S. Blanco, 'Origin and History of the Plot of *Marianela*', *Hispania* (U.S.A.), 48 (1965), 463-67. Unconvincing claim that Charles Nodier's 'Les Aveugles de Chomanouny', published in his *Contes de la Veillée*, and Wilkie Collins's *Poor Miss Finch* were chief sources.

37. Peter A. Bly, 'Egotism and Charity in *Marianela*', *AG*, 7 (1972), 49-66. Interesting but overstates Galdós's hostility to material progress.

38. Juan Cruz Mendizábal, 'Los ciegos: la otra realidad, los ojos matan', *Letras de Deusto*, 8 (1978), 59-75. Uninspired, descriptive account of the contrast between the ideal and the real.

39. Brian J. Dendle, 'Shipwreck and Discovery: A Study of Imagery in *Marianela*', *Neuphilologische Mitteilungen*, 74 (1973), 326-32. Persuasively argues that the imagery expresses Galdós's desire to reconcile the spiritual and the material.

40. ——, 'Galdós, Ayguals de Izco, and the Hellenic Inspiration of *Marianela*', in *Galdós Studies II*, ed. Robert J. Weber (London: Tamesis, 1974), pp.1-11. Dubious claim that Ayguals de Izco was chief source, but a useful corrective to Ruiz's (*52*) interpretation of role of Platonic doctrine.

41. Otis Green, 'Two Deaths: Don Quijote and Marianela', *AG*, 2 (1967), 131-33. Suggests Galdós based the death scene on that of Don Quijote.

42. C.A. Jones, 'Galdós's *Marianela* and the Approach to Reality', *Modern Language Review*, 56 (1961), 515-19. Lucidly-argued refutation of Casalduero's Comtian interpretation.

43. Ernesto Krebs, *'Marianela' y 'Doña Bárbara': ensayo de comparación* (Bahía Blanca: Cuadernos del Sur, Instituto de Humanidades, Universidad Nacional del Sur, 1967), pp.11-111. Broad, discursive study with no critical apparatus but with some interesting insights.

44. John Thomas Lister, 'Symbolism in *Marianela*', *Hispania* (U.S.A.), 14 (1931), 347-50. Simplistic symbolic interpretation.

45. José López Muñoz, 'Felipe Centeno, un héroe oscuro e inédito', *Papeles de Son Armadans*, 73 (1974), 249-58. Brief survey of evolution of Felipe's character in three novels.

46. Luis Lozano, '*Marianela* de Galdós y *La Sinfonía pastoral* de Gide',
     Letras de Deusto, 4 (1974), 225-38. Unenlightening comparison.

47. '*Marianela*', *Benito Pérez Galdós*, Compendio Vosgos, 38 (Barcelona:
     Vosgos, 1978). Unsophisticated and tendentious introduction;
     chapter-by-chapter synopsis and commentary.

48. Eugenio Matus, 'Sobre *Doña Perfecta* y *Marianela*', *Estudios
     Filológicos*, 6 (1970), 135-49. Interesting comparison of themes and
     styles.

49. Teresa Méndez Faith, 'Del sentimiento caritativo en *Marianela* y
     Misericordia', *Bulletin Hispanique*, 84 (1982), 420-33. Adds little to
     Bly's more comprehensive study (*37*).

50. Walter T. Pattison, *Benito Pérez Galdós and the Creative Process*
     (Minneapolis: University of Minnesota Press, 1954), pp.114-50.
     Important study of influence of Goethe, Hugo, and Sue, but exaggerates
     Galdós's debt.

51. Roberto Peraire Vidal, '*Marianela*', '*Miau*': *análisis, estudio crítico y
     comentarios*, Colección Resumen y Comentarios, 27 (Río Piedras:
     Edil, 1984). Chapter-by-chapter summary and brief, largely derivative,
     critical comments.

52. Mario E. Ruiz, 'El idealismo platónico en *Marianela* de Galdós',
     Hispania (U.S.A.), 53 (1970), 870-80. Important article which
     identifies Platonic elements but reaches questionable conclusions.

53. Marie A. Wellington, '*Marianela*: nuevas dimensiones', *Hispania*
     (U.S.A.), 51 (1968), 38-48. Thought-provoking article which modifies
     Casalduero's Comtian interpretation (*12*).

54. ——, '*Marianela* de Galdós y Diderot', *CHA*, no.324 (1977), 558-69.
     Ultimately unsuccessful attempt to establish Diderot's *Lettre sur les
     aveugles* and *Traité du beau* as sources.

55. ——, '*Marianela* and *La Symphonie pastorale*', in *Romance Literary
     Studies: Homage to Harvey L. Johnson,* ed. Marie E. Wellington and
     Martha O'Nan (Potomac, Maryland: Studia Humanitatis, 1979), 169-71.
     Claims Gide knew *Marianela*.

56. ——, 'A Symbolism linking *Marianela* with the Torquemada Novels',
     Hispanófila, no.73 (1981), 21-27. Comparative study of the symbolical
     implications of blindness.

57. ——, '*Marianela* a la sombra de la realidad', in '*Marianela*': *escencia y
     espejo: cinco ensayos* (New York: Senda Nueva de Ediciones, 1984),
     pp.65-79. (This collection also contains reprints of *53*, *54*, *55* and *56*
     above. References in this Critical Guide are to the original publications).
     Unconvincing claim that the contemporary debates on slavery,
     especially speeches of Castelar, were sources, and ingenious
     interpretation of novel as allegory of relationship between Spain and
     Cuba.

I. THE NOVEL AND THE DRAMATIC VERSION

58. Rodolfo Cardona, '*Marianela*: su trayectoria de la novela al teatro', in
    Homenaje a Casalduero (Madrid: Gredos, 1972), pp.109-14.
    Reproduces two letters from Valle-Inclán and an outline, in Galdós's
    handwriting, for the dramatization of the novel.
59. Julio Casares, 'Desde la novela al teatro: *Marianela* de Pérez Galdós',
    in his *Obras completas*, 2nd ed. (Madrid: Espasa-Calpe, 1944), pp.31-44.
    Some sharp perceptions.

CRITICAL GUIDES TO SPANISH TEXTS

Edited by
J.E. Varey and A.D. Deyermond